Backpack To Briefcase

Steps to a Successful Career

2nd Edition

A Life After Graduation, LLC Publication

P.O. Box 11205 • Bainbridge Island WA 98110

(877) 569-9816 • Info@LifeAfterGraduation.com

www.LifeAfterGraduation.com

COPYRIGHT INFORMATION

BOOK DISCLAIMER

ACKNOWLEDGMENTS

Life After Graduation, LLC would like to acknowledge and thank the thousands of colleges, instructors and students who have made *Backpack To Briefcase* a success. We would also like to acknowledge and thank the following reviewers for their insightful suggestions regarding the revision of this new edition:

Ms. Debbie Edwards, Director of Career Services
Washington State University

Ms. Minda Heyman, Associate Director of Career Development
Goucher College

Ms. Nancie Merritt, Human Resources Consultant, Sr.
Insurance Services Office, Inc.

Mr. Phillip Ronniger, Career Counselor
Washington State University

Ms. Linda Taylor, Director of Student Support Services
Murray State College

Ms. Tonya Thompson, Coordinator of Career Services
Clarion University – Venango Campus

Terry Arndt
President
Life After Graduation, LLC

Table of Contents

Backpack To Briefcase

Introduction

Backpack To Briefcase

Congratulations! You have your degree, a job (or at least a lot of job prospects), a wealth of skills and knowledge, and – as a new graduate – plenty of enthusiasm. What you need now is a resource to guide you through the challenges you will encounter during your career. That's what **Backpack To Briefcase** is for.

This is an exciting time. The possibilities are limitless and your future is, more than ever, completely up to you. The more you know about how to manage your career; the better off you'll be – now and in the long run.

Whether your first job is a dream position on the management team of a Fortune 500 company or an entry-level position at a local marketing firm, you need to know what to expect and – perhaps more importantly – how to deal with the unexpected. **Backpack To Briefcase** will help you navigate these early days of your career by providing you:

- Tips on how to create and maintain a professional image.

- Advice on workplace etiquette.

- Strategies to successfully handle all areas of work life, from business functions and work communications to working on teams and handling mistakes and missteps in the office.

- Need-to-know information regarding your benefits, your paycheck and your rights as an employee.

- Pointers on people and personalities that will help make your interactions with co-workers and supervisors positive.

- Essential career advice to help you excel in your profession, including how to network effectively and how to choose a mentor.

- Guidance for dealing with the unpredictable aspects of work life, such as personality conflicts, awkward situations, and layoffs.

- And much, much more.

Backpack To Briefcase is designed to answer all the questions you have – and some you might not have even thought of yet! It will not only guide you through the first days at your new job, it will also teach you the intricacies of successfully completing a performance review and asking for a raise.

Now get ready to leave that backpack behind, pick up that briefcase, and let's get your career on the path to success!

Chapter 1

Your Professional Image

Maybe you've never thought about your "professional image," but you can be sure that your new boss, coworkers and clients will be thinking about it – a lot. In fact, despite the old advice to "never judge a book by its cover," people interpret the image you project as a reflection of your abilities, character, and value as an employee.

While some are able to look past initial appearances and see others for their skills, commitment, intelligence, and value to the workplace, most form opinions of one another the moment they meet – and these opinions are usually based on superficial characteristics like clothing, mannerisms and speech. Quite simply, we judge what we see. By getting to know someone we learn to look beyond the surface. But once a negative impression is made, we do not get a second chance. That's why first impressions are important – if someone believes you are unprofessional because you wore wrinkled pants to your first day of work or used the word "dude" one too many times during an early encounter, you will have to work twice as hard to change his or her opinion of you.

Think about the kind of professional image you would like to project. Are you trustworthy? Committed? Educated and skilled? Creative? Hardworking? Dependable? What kind of image do you project right now, at this moment, through your outward appearance and other tangible characteristics like speech, mannerisms and style? Are these two images – the one you project now and the one you would like to project – similar? If not, why not? What do you need to change in order to reconcile the two images and create the kind of professional image that fits your needs?

What is a Professional Image?

To create your ideal professional image, you must first understand exactly what a professional image is. Simply put, your professional image is the collection of qualities and characteristics that influence the opinions of others – namely your supervisors, co-workers and clients. These qualities and characteristics include things that may be very obvious to you – and others that you may never have imagined, including:

- Attire
- Make-up, jewelry, hairstyle
- Grooming
- Speech, including regional accents, vocabulary and grammar
- Mannerisms
- Posture
- Subjects you talk about, or interests/hobbies/opinions you reveal
- How you decorate your desk
- How messy or how clean your workspace is
- Things/people that can be attributed to you, including your car, your home, your friends and family
- Groups and organizations with which you associate yourself
- Your behavior. For example, are you always late or always on-time? Do you laugh a lot or are you more serious? Are you friendly and engaging or shy and aloof?
- Habits (i.e., bad ones like smoking and nail biting, or good ones like exercising)

In the workplace, as in life, people observe you and form opinions about who you are. Your career success relies at least in part on this fact. Therefore, it is in your best interest to manage your image so that people are led to believe what you want them to believe about you. The following chapters will assist you with this process.

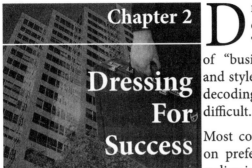

Chapter 2

Dressing For Success

Dressing for work used to be easier: you wore a suit. Period. These days, however, in the age of "business casual," "casual Friday," and styles that are constantly changing, decoding the office dress code can be difficult.

Most companies have a written policy on preferred or required attire. This policy isn't necessarily written in stone, but it's a good place to start. Familiarize yourself with the policy: Does it make suggestions for standard dress? Does it list items that are absolutely not allowed – shorts, hats, open-toed shoes, for example? Does it mention "casual Friday"? In the earliest days of your employment, it's best to follow the guidelines laid out in the policy – and keep in mind that it's better to be a little overdressed than underdressed.

More conservative professions, like banking and law, tend to have stricter, more conservative expectations about dress. On the other hand, more creative fields, like graphic design, advertising or publishing, often grant more leeway – and may even encourage personal flair and cutting-edge style. Here are some guidelines:

- Even if your company has a fairly relaxed dress code, you will usually need to dress up on days when you will be greeting or meeting with clients.

- Casual doesn't mean sloppy. Even if your workplace is very casual, don't wear wrinkled, dirty, stained, torn or faded clothing.

- Don't be the first to break a dress code rule or push the style envelope. If your supervisors start wearing open-toed shoes or jeans on Friday on a regular basis, it's probably okay, but wait until they take the lead.

- Avoid wearing clothing with symbols, writing or artwork that is overtly religious, political, risqué or crass. Work is not the place to wear your "Libertarian and Proud" jacket or the t-shirt from your favorite bar with the off-color saying.

- Anything revealing, low-cut or overly tight is out of the question for work.

- No matter how casual your workplace is, flip-flops, sweatpants, baseball hats and shorts are never a good option. You want to project a professional image no matter what everybody else is wearing.

Maintaining Your Personal Style

Dressing for work can sometimes feel like you're wearing a uniform, but it doesn't have to. Following a dress code doesn't mean you have to completely abandon your individuality. In fact, showing some creativity, style and personal flair may just get you noticed – as long as you do it right.

- Play with color and pattern. A neutral, mix-and-match palate is a great way to establish a work wardrobe, but once your budget allows, splurge on a suit in a great color or pattern.

- Accessories are a safe and inexpensive way to express some style. Think one-of-a-kind jewelry, a tie in a trendy pattern, shoes in the latest style, or a stand-out belt.

- Bags, purses and briefcases are a great place to show personal flair. Because you don't wear them all day long, you can take more of a chance with them, going a little brighter, trendier or wild. The same goes for coats.

- Every so often, buy a fashion magazine and browse the pages looking for professional yet stylish looks you admire. Try to copy these looks on a budget by shopping sales and discount stores.

- Spend some time in clothing stores at the start of every season to get a sense for the latest styles and trends, then add a few pieces each season that you feel fit your personal style *and* your office dress code.

Dressing Up on a Budget

No doubt you would love to dress in the latest fashions and in the best designers and labels. But, as a new graduate, you're most likely on a fairly restricted budget – and a professional-quality wardrobe doesn't come cheap. Keep in mind the following tips while developing your wardrobe:

- **Plan Well** – Make a list of what clothing you would like to purchase for work and begin shopping early, rather than waiting until last minute and making hasty decisions. Give yourself the time to comparison shop, research sales, and make informed and careful choices that fit your budget and personal style.

- **Start with Neutrals** – Navy, black, tan and taupe are great choices for key wardrobe pieces that can then be jazzed up with accessories in bright colors and great patterns.

- **Stick to Classics** – Trendy is fun, but investing in wardrobe pieces that will serve you well over time makes more sense. Women can't go wrong with high-quality leather pumps in a neutral color, skirts or pant suits in simple cuts, and sweater sets. Men should look for neutral suits in a classic style, high-quality lace-up dress shoes, leather belts, solid color dress shirts and conservative ties in the classic medium width.

- **Buy Quality Over Quantity** – Buying one great, high-end suit with a great fit and changing its look with different shirts and accessories will make a better impression than buying several poor-quality, ill-fitting suits that look cheap. Plus, quality lasts longer. Spending more up front for a good but expensive pair of shoes that will last is smarter than buying a cheap pair that wear badly over time and have to be replaced in a few months. If you must buy inexpensive pieces, remember that poor quality is less evident in solids, classic cuts and neutral colors.

- **Consider the Fabric** – Try to choose fabrics that can be worn in all seasons and that travel well without wrinkling. Also consider whether pieces need to be dry cleaned or not: a sweater set that can be hand-washed and hung to dry is more budget conscious than the set that has to be dry cleaned.

- **Accessorize** – Carefully chosen and stylish accessories can turn a ho-hum neutral outfit into a stunner and can make the same suit look different from day to day. Women: consider tasteful but striking jewelry, scarves, shoes and bags. Men: think about a quality watch, stylish and colorful ties, and good belts and shoes.

- **Build Your Wardrobe Slowly** – Save your money to buy a few high-quality pieces each year, and keep an eye out for great but low-cost accessories that emphasize your personal style, such as jewelry and ties. With careful planning and good choices, you will have a workable professional wardrobe within the first few years of your professional life.

- **Consider Second-Hand and Consignment Stores** – Every metropolitan area has a range of great "nearly new" stores that often stock high-end, designer clothing that has been gently worn. Also shop outlets, sales and discount stores.

Looking Your Best

So you've got your wardrobe down and know how to dress. What else matters? A lot. Dressing the part is the foundation of a professional look, but there are other things to consider as well. Remember:

- Grooming is important. Get regular haircuts, keep your nails clean and groomed, shave as often as needed, and make sure you are always clean.

- Keep jewelry simple and minimal.

- If you have tattoos, make sure they are covered – not everybody thinks they are stylish and appealing.

- The same goes for piercings. If you have piercings that are visible, you should remove them. Some of the artistic and creative fields may allow piercings, but until you are sure, it's better to be safe than sorry.

- Women should wear make-up if they feel it makes them look their best; however, it should be minimal and tasteful.

- Hairstyles should be stylish yet not outlandish. If you haven't changed your hair since middle school, it's probably time for an update. On the other hand, your first day of work isn't the time to try out a mohawk or the latest super-trendy look.

- Long hair on men is generally not recommended; super-long hair on women isn't either.

- Remember that you want to be viewed as an adult. Evaluate your look for anything that might seem too young or childish. A few examples might include high school rings, Hello Kitty purses, or clothing embroidered with your fraternity or sorority letters.

- Shoes are important. Make sure they are in good shape, with no scuffs, rips or holes.

- Perfume is a very personal choice; therefore, don't wear strong scents that might offend or bother your co-workers. If people can smell you coming, you're wearing too much!

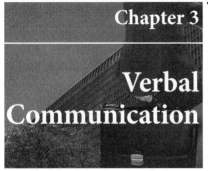

Chapter 3

Verbal Communication

We spend a large portion of every day talking. It's how we make our needs and wants known, get our messages across, and share our humor, knowledge and values. Yet the way we speak and what we say is often overlooked as an important part of our image. Don't underestimate the importance of good verbal communication skills to your professional success – they are critically important.

Communication Styles

Communication styles can be influenced by a variety of factors, such as culture, gender, personality, and education. Everyone has his or her own personal style. Understanding your own style as well as the different types you might encounter in others will give you an advantage in communicating with a broad range of people and will help you communicate more clearly. Here are some tips on managing communication styles:

- Ask yourself what parts of your communication style are working for you and where you can improve.

- If you find you have difficulty communicating with a person, evaluate his/her communication style and think about how and why it clashes with your own. Then, come up with some strategies for dealing with it.

- Ask a friend, family member, or even a supervisor (in a performance review, for example) to evaluate your communication style and give you feedback.

Grammar and Vocabulary

Use good grammar and a developed vocabulary, and people will say you are well spoken and articulate. They'll also see you as intelligent, educated and capable. Use poor grammar and exercise a limited vocabulary and people will believe just the opposite.

There's really no proof that good grammar and vocabulary are indicators of high intelligence or advanced degrees, but the way a person speaks will definitely impact the impression he/she leaves with the listener. Communicate the right message by following these simple recommendations.

- Reading is a great way to develop your vocabulary. Make a point of reading at least one magazine or newspaper a week and try to read a few books a year as well.

- If someone uses a word with which you are unfamiliar, make a mental note of it and look it up later. The same goes for words you might encounter while reading. Keep a dictionary on your desk for just this reason.

- If you are not sure of the meaning or usage of a word, don't use it. Better to use simple, but correct, language than to try to impress someone with a big word and get it wrong.

- Nobody is impressed by lingo, the use of big words or the use of obscure language for the sake of impressing people. Your goal should be to speak clearly and communicate your message – not to confound or confuse people with your intelligence.

- Vary the words you use. Using the same word too much causes the word to lose its power. For example, if you say that everything is extraordinary, from the way your lunch tastes to the fact that you just landed a big client, people will begin to realize that you don't actually mean anything when you say something is extraordinary.

- If you are unable to judge your grammar and vocabulary skills on your own, ask a friend or family member to observe you over the course of a day or an evening and give you feedback on what they notice about your linguistic strengths and weaknesses.

- If you are not confident in your grammar and vocabulary skills, buy a book on the subject or enroll in a basic course. Community centers and colleges often offer classes in English for just this purpose.

Common Grammar Mistakes

Wrong Verb Tense

Incorrect: I **seen** Jim yesterday.
Correct: I **saw** Jim yesterday.

Subject-Verb Agreement

Incorrect: The **captain** of the fleet of ships **don't** like losing.

Correct: The **captain** of the fleet of ships **doesn't** like losing.

Good vs. Well

Incorrect: She cooks **good.**

Correct: She cooks **well.**

TIP: *Good is an adjective that describes a noun, while well is an adverb that describes a verb. So, someone is a good singer (because good is describing the noun "singer"), but someone sings* well *(because well is describing how someone sings – a verb).*

Lay vs. Lie

Correct: After I **lay** the computer keyboard on my desk,
I will **lie** down and rest.

Me vs. I

Incorrect: Tom and **me** went to lunch.

Correct: Tom and **I** went to lunch.

TIP: *Take the other person out of the sentence and see if it makes sense. For example – would you say "Me went to lunch"? Of course not – so you should use* I.

Who vs. Whom

Incorrect: To **who** did you give the money?

Correct: To **whom** did you give the money?

Don't vs. Doesn't.

Incorrect: He **don't** care about anything.

Correct: He **doesn't** care about anything

Bring vs. Take

Incorrect: When we go to the meeting, let's **bring** our laptops.

Correct: When we go to the meeting, let's **take** our laptops.

Less vs. Fewer

Incorrect: Ten items or **less**

Correct: Ten items or **fewer**

TIP: *If you can't count the substance, you should use* less. *With things that can be counted, use* fewer.

Of vs. Have

Incorrect: I would **of** thought you'd be happy.

Correct: I would **have** thought you'd be happy.

Double Negative

Incorrect:	I'm **not** inviting **nobody** to the meeting.
Correct:	I'm **not** inviting **anybody** to the meeting.

Present Perfect

Incorrect:	I **would have took** a taxi.
Correct:	I **would have taken** a taxi.

Slang

Slang is defined as: *casual or playful language used by a subculture or group of people to express meaning or attitude in a word.*

Just about everyone has used slang at one time or another, and slang does have its place in society – just not in the workplace. For a young person working to establish him or herself in the workplace as mature, responsible and intelligent, the use of slang can be counterproductive. Some common examples of slang used by young people today include:

- Cool
- Like
- Awesome
- Right on
- You guys
- Dude
- No problemo
- Man

While at the office, avoid using slang. Unfortunately, the use of slang is often something of a habit that can be difficult to break. In fact, you may even be surprised to learn how often you do use it. To break the slang habit:

- Observe yourself and take note. The first step to stopping slang-talk is to become aware of when you are using the language so you can make a conscious effort to stop. If you are unable to do it on you own, ask a friend to spend the day pointing out to you whenever you use a slang word.

- Understand that people from different age groups and cultures may misunderstand slang and find it annoying.

- Know that slang is like a language shortcut. For example, if your supervisor praises you for your work on a recent project and you respond, "cool," you are missing the opportunity to say what you actually mean which is probably something more along the lines of, "Thank you for noticing my success. I worked really hard on that project and learned a lot. In fact, I can't wait to be assigned another challenging project like that so I can continue to prove my abilities and grow as an employee."

- If you find it difficult to quit using slang, create a cessation strategy. For example, put a rubber band around your wrist and snap it every time you catch yourself using slang. Reward yourself with a small gift when you can make it through the day without snapping the rubber band more than two or three times.

Listening

When it comes to communication, there's a reason we have two ears and only one mouth. Being a good communicator is being a good listener, yet many people sorely lack good listening skills. That's right – listening is a skill, and one you need to practice in order to master. True listening is an active, three-step process that includes:

- **Hearing** – The act of taking in the words and the sensory experience of someone speaking to you.

- **Understanding** – The process of taking what you have heard and giving it meaning and context that makes sense to you.

- **Judging** – The process of assigning opinion and value to what you've heard and understood from the communication. For example, do you believe what you have heard? Do you think it's true?

Here are some basic tips for practicing good, active listening:

- Give your full attention to the speaker.

- Focus. Don't let your mind wander or try to guess what the person will say next.

- Don't interrupt.

- Don't use the time while the other person is speaking to formulate what you will say in response. If you do, you're not really listening.

- Listen for main ideas.

- Ask questions.

- Give feedback. Use your body posture, expressions and words to let the other person know you are listening and give them an indication of how you feel about what they are saying. For example, nodding can show agreement, while cocking your head can indicate confusion.

Public Speaking

For some people, speaking in front of a group of people is enough to induce a panic attack. Others thrive on being the center of attention. One thing is for sure – at one time or another, nearly everyone will find it necessary to speak publicly. From presenting a report at a meeting, to giving a speech at a conference, to making a toast at a work celebration, public speaking is something you will have to do. Even if you aren't a natural at public speaking, you can employ a few simple strategies to make sure that you communicate well and keep your cool.

- Be familiar with the place where you will be speaking – it will make you more comfortable. If necessary, arrive early and check out your podium, microphone, etc.

- Get to know the audience. If you know you will be speaking at a conference, greet people as they arrive. It's easier to speak in front of people who are familiar than in front of a group of total strangers.

- Know your material.

- Relax.

- Use visualization to ensure success. Visualize yourself speaking clearly, loudly and slowly.

- Understand that people want you to succeed. Your audience isn't hoping that you'll be boring or embarrass yourself. Knowing this will put you at ease.

- Don't draw attention to your nervousness by apologizing. If you don't say anything about problems that might arise, the audience might not even notice.

- Concentrate on your message – not on your nervousness.

- Turn your nervousness into excitement and enthusiasm.

- Gain experience. Even though it might not appeal to you, take every chance you can to practice public speaking. For example, offer to give the Thanksgiving blessing at your family dinner or a toast at a friend's wedding. The more you do it, the better you'll get.

Keeping Private Matters Private

You know the cliché: some things are better left unsaid. That's especially true when it comes to work and certain subjects. Although you may become very comfortable and friendly with people at work, you should keep some subjects private. Use discretion: it's a good rule of thumb to remember that if you wouldn't want the boss to know it about you, you probably shouldn't let anyone else at work know either. Subjects to keep off limits at work include:

- **Religion** – Religion is a personal choice and a private matter and really has no place in the office. You don't have to keep the fact that you belong to a specific religious group a secret, but you shouldn't be preaching, trying to influence others religious opinions, or judging people for their own religious beliefs, either.

- **Politics** – Politics, like religion, is a personal choice and one that most people feel very strongly about. Political debates can get very heated and are inappropriate for the office.

- **Romance** – It's fine to talk with co-workers you consider friends about who you are dating – but keep the details of your latest romantic encounters to yourself. In general, just be tasteful and discreet about what you say at work when it comes to matters of the heart.

- **Illegal Activities** – It goes without saying that you shouldn't be doing anything illegal anyway, but if you do, you should zip your lips about it at work. Past or current drug use, drinking and driving, prior arrests – none of these reflect well on you, so you shouldn't make them known.

- **Money** – Nobody needs to know how much money you make, how you spend it, or how much specific items that you own cost – and you shouldn't ask your co-workers about any of these things, either.

- **Health** – Unless you want to reveal it, you don't have to let anyone know about any health conditions you might have. Assume people do not want to hear the details of your latest medical procedure or the disgusting symptoms of your bout with the flu. By the same token, it's none of your business why your office mate takes a pill every day after lunch – no matter how curious you might be.

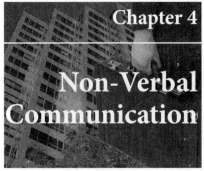

Chapter 4

Non-Verbal Communication

Speaking isn't the only way that you talk to people. In fact, some communication experts believe that up to 95 percent of our communication is expressed non-verbally. Think about it – if someone says "Very nice to meet you," but she's scowling, has her hands crossed stiffly across her chest, and doesn't offer her hand to shake, what is she actually saying? In the workplace, as in life, non-verbal communication is a huge part of how we actually talk to each other. Make sure you're saying the right things by following these tips.

The Handshake

The handshake is an important form of non-verbal communication used in the workplace. It's often the first form of communication between two people, and is therefore a vital part of making a positive first impression. Here's how to get it right:

- Know when handshakes are appropriate. Generally, handshakes are welcome when greeting someone for the first time or someone you have not seen in a while, when congratulating someone, or when saying goodbye to someone you may not see for an extended period of time.

- Make sure your hand will be comfortable to shake. It should be clean, dry and not too cold.

- Carry things in your left hand when you are expecting to be shaking hands. For example, when at a business party, carry your drink in your left hand. When entering a business meeting, carry your briefcase or documents in your left hand.

- Allow someone who may have difficulty with or may not be accustomed to handshakes to initiate the action. For example, someone who is disabled and has difficulty moving his arms, someone whose hands are full, or someone from a different country or culture where handshaking may not be the norm.

- Make eye contact and smile during the handshake.

- Extend your hand confidently and shake firmly, but not too vigorously. Firmly grasp the other person's hand so that the web between your thumb and forefinger is touching their web.

- Shake two or three times at most, then release.

- Be discreet should the other person not notice you have extended your hand, or if he/she is not responsive to your effort to shake their hand. Don't embarrass someone who misses your cues to shake his/her hand.

- Apologize should there be a reason that you cannot shake hands. For example, if your hands are full or wet, or if you are sick and do not want to spread germs.

Posture

Good posture can help you exude confidence – while poor posture can do exactly the opposite. Developing good posture is not only good for your health, it can also help you communicate a positive image with your body. When standing, you should stand tall with your back straight, chest out, shoulders pulled back and arms to your sides. In addition:

- When entering a room, always take a moment to consider your posture. Ask yourself what your posture is communicating, then make adjustments as necessary.

- Avoid locking your knees and standing straight up and down – it can look awkward. If necessary, take some time at home to stand in front of a mirror and observe how different postures look and feel.

- When speaking to a person, lean forward toward him/her slightly to appear interested.

- Avoid crossing your arms or clasping your hands in front of your body.

- If you have difficulty keeping your hands at your side, hold a pen or other appropriate object to give your hands something to do and to remind you to keep your arms at your side.

- Avoid leaning against furniture or the wall – it can give the appearance that you are lazy or bored.

- When sitting, don't "plop" into a chair – ease into it by lowering yourself slowly into sitting position.

- If your chair has arms, rest your arms on them. If not, rest your hands in your lap.

- Sit up straight, don't slouch.

- When in a serious environment, keep both feet on the ground. More casual environments may allow you to cross your legs. Don't cross your legs if it affects good posture, however.

- When walking, walk with your head held high and your chin tucked in slightly. If your chin is held too high, however, it can give you the appearance of being unapproachable.

- Walk with purpose and direction.

- Walk fairly quickly so as not to give the appearance that you are meandering and not attending to your work.

Gestures and Expressions

If eyes are windows to the soul and a look can say a thousand words, then you'd do well to pay attention to what yours are saying! Gestures and facial expressions can help us communicate – and they can also betray us if we aren't careful. Keep the following in mind:

- Facial expressions provide obvious clues to a person's interest level, understanding and confidence.

- Make eye contact when communicating; however, continuous eye contact can be construed as aggressive and can make others uncomfortable.

- Avoid being distracted by things going on around you and looking away while communicating. Doing so is disrespectful and gives the impression that you are not interested.

- Smile. It makes you seem approachable, confident and interested.

- If necessary, observe your facial expressions in a mirror at home and practice until you are comfortable using your expressions as a means of communication.

- Try to keep your hand gestures smooth and flowing. Sudden or jerky movements can be distracting.

- Vary the gestures you use. Using gestures too often can make them lose their effectiveness.

- If necessary, ask a friend to observe you while using gestures and give you feedback on their effectiveness.

Personal Space

Distance and space are important factors to keep in mind as you interact with others. Speaking to someone too closely may make the person feel you are invading his/her personal space and can be construed as aggressive or annoying. On the other hand, creating too much of a distance can also be uncomfortable and awkward. Keep in mind:

- In the United States it is customary to maintain a distance of at least three to four feet between yourself and another person while speaking.

- Space requirements among other cultures may be different. If you will be communicating with people from other countries and cultures, do some research to find out what kind of personal space they maintain.

- Some circumstances – such as a crowded room – may require you to adjust your distance and personal space accordingly.

- Always knock before entering another person's work space and wait to be offered a seat before being seated.

- If a person is in a conversation or on the phone when you enter his/her workspace, keep an appropriate distance or come back at another time so as not to appear to be eavesdropping.

- When conversing with someone who is seated, place yourself in a position so that you can easily maintain eye contact.

Chapter 5

Communication Devices

Today, there are many ways to send a message including the telephone, the Internet, or the letter. Good communication is the foundation of success at work, but it's not always easy to accomplish. As Al Ries, legendary marketing strategist and bestselling business author, once said, "Today, communication itself is the problem. We have become the world's first overcommunicated society. Each year we send more and receive less."

Several studies have shown that Al Ries is correct. Poor communication skills have cost businesses billions of dollars in wasted time and resources. Use the strategies and skills described in this chapter to efficiently and effectively communicate.

Telephone Communication

The phone is an essential tool of modern business life. And, while you've been using a phone for most of your life, there's a unique business etiquette for telephone use. Make your telephone communications as professional, efficient and effective as possible by following these tips and suggestions:

- Answer calls on the second ring. Answering a phone the moment it rings will make you seem too eager and catch the caller off guard; waiting too long can make the caller impatient or angry.

- Answer calls with a professional and friendly greeting that includes your company's name and your name. For example, "Good morning, XYZ Company, John Doe speaking, may I help you?"

- Smile during calls – it may sound funny, but a smile actually affects the way you speak and will make you seem friendlier, even over the phone lines.

- Ask callers for their name – even if it doesn't seem necessary. This indicates that you have taken an interest in the caller. After you know the caller's name, use it during the course of the conversation.

- Speak clearly and slowly.

- Avoid chewing gum or eating while on the phone.

- Speak at an appropriate volume. If you normally speak loudly, lower your voice. Those who speak softly should raise their voice so the caller can hear them easily.

- Keep the phone about the width of two fingers from your mouth so as not to muffle your speech.

- Ask the caller if it is okay to do so before you put them on hold, then thanking them for holding once you return.

- Transfer callers to the appropriate person if necessary, instead of transferring them to the operator or telling them to call another extension. Let the caller know that you are transferring them, to whom you are transferring them, and why.

- Take effective messages for others by including the caller's name and company, time and date of call, subject of call, if and when the caller wants a return phone call, and a phone number at which the caller can be reached.

- End calls with a pleasantry such as "Have a nice day," or "Thank you for calling."

- Let the caller hang up first so you don't seem overly eager to end the call.

Voice Mail Messages

In your work life, you may sometimes find that you leave more messages than you have telephone conversations! Gone are the days of busy signals and never-ending phone rings – just about every phone call you make has the potential to end with leaving a message, so you better be prepared.

When leaving a voice mail message:

- Be brief and get to the point immediately.

- Be pleasant and polite.

- Speak in a clear, concise manner. You want to ensure the listener is able to hear your message.

- Include, at the very minimum, the date and time of your call, your name, a return phone number, and the subject or reason for the call.

- Put your call in context. For example, "This is John Doe. We met at the trade show last week in Phoenix and discussed potential new business products."

- Give the caller a reason to call you back. For example, "Please call me back so we can continue our great discussion on new business products and possibly move forward with the new product."

- If necessary, let the caller know when you need the phone call returned by, and what the consequences of not returning the call might be. For example, "This is Jane Doe from accounting. I need you to call me by 5 p.m. today to discuss the bill of your client, Mr. Smith. If I don't speak with you today, I won't be able to bill Mr. Smith until the next billing cycle, which will put your account in the past due category."

- Finish your message by repeating your name and telephone number.

When developing your own voice mail message:

- Be brief.

- Establish your identity immediately. For example, "Hello, you have reached the desk of John Doe."

- Sound friendly and positive. Nobody wants to listen to a message that sounds like it was recorded by someone who would rather be anywhere else but at work.

- Tell the caller what to do. For example, "Please state your name, your phone number and the reason for your call."

- Give other options, if possible. Some callers want to hear a human voice. If you can, tell callers that if they need help immediately to push a certain extension to transfer them to the operator, an administrative assistant, or a co-worker that is familiar with your clients and work. Or, give them another way or reaching you, like your cell phone or beeper. This method also cuts down on the number of messages you will receive, so you won't have to wade through multiple messages every time you step away from your desk. Just make sure it's okay with the person to whom you are transferring calls.

- Indicate in your message when you will be available. For example, if you are away on business or vacation, let the caller know in your message that you are out of the office and when you will be returning.

Personal Calls

Because the phone is such a vital communication tool, you may not think twice about picking it up to call a friend or family member during work hours. But think again. Most companies allow a certain number of personal phone calls during business hours – after all, we do have lives beyond the office walls and sometimes need to check in on children or elderly parents, confirm dinner plans with friends, or take care of a pressing situation with our homes or personal lives. But be aware that personal calls are just that – personal – and should be kept to a minimum.

In most states, calls made from a place of business can be recorded and monitored, although most of the time you must be made aware that calls are being recorded. Your employer will also most likely have access to records of phone calls made and received at your phone extension. In most cases, phone use is not strictly monitored, but if a supervisor begins to notice or is tipped off by a co-worker that your personal phone use is excessive, you might be subject to more scrutiny. And, in certain businesses, like customer service or government contracting with security clearance issues, phone calls may be more closely monitored.

It's a good policy to use your own cell phone or a pay phone for personal calls during your lunch hour or other breaks. Keep personal calls on business phones to a minimum, and only for emergencies or very short calls with completely benign subject matter. Never discuss sensitive matters on business phones and don't make personal long-distance phone calls from work.

Electronic Communication

Most companies have Web sites to help consumers find them, and many larger companies have developed company "Intranet" sites to serve as a communications resource for employees where they can find out about company news, employee benefits, and other company-related information. Now, nearly unlimited information is at your fingertips and you can communicate within seconds to someone halfway across the world. With these advances come amazing conveniences and possibilities – and also a whole new set of rules and strategies. Here's how to use electronic means of communication:

E-mail Etiquette

You probably use e-mail with friends and family and are very comfortable using it as a way to communicate. However, don't get too comfortable. Writing an e-mail to your boss or a client should be approached much differently than writing a friend. When writing a business e-mail, remember:

- In general, use the standards of good business writing (see the *Written Communication* section in this chapter).

- Ask yourself why you are writing the e-mail message. Do you need the recipient to take action or provide you information? Do you need to provide information? If you can't state why you are writing the message, don't send a message. People receive dozens, hundreds, sometimes even thousands of e-mail messages every week. Don't add to the clutter by sending unnecessary messages.

- Be brief and get to the point right away. E-mail is great because it's quick and easy. Make sure your e-mail messages are quick and easy, too. If an e-mail message become lengthy, requires detailed or extensive action from the audience, or contains important or sensitive information, you need to employ another mode of communication – such as a business letter, memo or report.

- Give e-mails useful subject lines. Let your readers know what the e-mail is about. Avoid empty subject lines like "Hi" or "FYI."

- Don't mix content. Don't put a reminder about the fun lunch on Friday in with an important request for a client proposal. The important information just might get lost. If you need to address two different subjects, send two different e-mails.

- Don't feel pressured to reply. If someone sends you an e-mail that needs no further action from you, don't respond with a "Thanks" or "Got it." That makes the other party feel like they must respond with "You're welcome," or "Great," – and the chain goes on.

- Write every e-mail as if your boss is reading it – she may do so. You never know who your e-mail will be forwarded to.

- Eliminate emotion. It's easy to write a terse reply and hit send – and then regret it an hour later. Conveying annoyance, anger or outright aggression in an e-mail is never a good idea. Let emotional e-mails sit for a few hours – chances are you will think better of it.

- Avoid tricky formatting. Plain text is fine.

- Avoid using cute abbreviations or symbols. Your friends might know that TTYL means "Talk to you later" but chances are your supervisor doesn't.

- Avoid large attachments. Downloading a large attachment can jam up some computers for 30 minutes or more. Don't aggravate your recipient – put large files on disk and deliver.

- Beware the "Reply All" button. When replying, you have two choices: Reply and Reply All. The reply response will generate a message to only the person who wrote the original e-mail. Reply All will send your reply message to every recipient of the original e-mail. So, for example, if a co-worker sends out a message to 40 colleagues informing them of a meeting, and you hit Reply All in response, all 40 of those people will get your "I'll be there," response. Unnecessary? Yes. Annoying? Definitely! Only use Reply All when it's appropriate.

- Include a signature. Every e-mail you send at work should include your name, title, your company name, your work phone number and your work e-mail address. Some companies even have standards for employee e-mail "signatures," and ask you to include a logo, a link to the company Web site, or other information. Recipients of your messages should know who you are, whom you work for and how to reach you – it's good business and it's good marketing for your company as well.

- Respond to your e-mail messages promptly, but don't check your e-mail Inbox continually throughout the day. This will only act as a distraction from other projects you are working on. Instead, set aside specific times during the day to read and respond to e-mails, such as first thing in the morning, after lunch and again before the end of the day. This will not only allow you to reply in a timely fashion, but also minimize distractions from other projects you are working on.

- Beware of unfamiliar e-mail address. Never open attachments from strange e-mail addresses. Sometimes viruses can even generate e-mails from real e-mail addresses in your e-mail address book. If an attachment looks strange or is unexpected, even from a known sender, call the sender to find out if it is legitimate.

Personal Use

The Internet and e-mail has revolutionized the business world, it's true, but there's another side to the story as well. Statistics show that worldwide, corporations lose billions in reduced productivity due to employee Internet use for non-work related purposes. According to Nielsen/NetRatings, 92 percent of online stock trading occurs from the workplace during work hours and 46 percent of online holiday shopping takes place at work! And, while most companies accept that employees will spend a limited amount of time on the Internet for personal reasons – checking their bank account balance or their personal e-mail account, for example – corporate America also realizes that personal Internet use can be a problem.

That's why more and more companies are shoring up their Internet use policies and spending both time and money to monitor the ways in which employees use the Internet. Companies are watching! And they don't necessarily do it just to be nosy. Employees that engage in illegal activity via the Internet also put their company at risk for legal action – or at the very least, public embarrassment. Plus, productivity can be significantly impacted by lax Internet use policies. Companies have every right to protect themselves by ensuring that employee Internet use is appropriate. Avoid potential conflicts by following these suggestions:

- Know your company's Internet use policies. Does your company frown on any use of the Internet at work? Or do they allow a limited amount of personal Internet use? Perhaps you can use the Internet for personal use, but only during your lunch hour. Does your company use a monitoring system? And what is the policy on handling inappropriate content that might be forwarded to you by a co-worker? Know the rules ahead of time and follow them.

- Limit personal Internet use or eliminate it altogether.

- Use the Internet for personal use as if your supervisor were looking over your shoulder. If you would be embarrassed if your supervisor saw the content you are viewing, you've crossed the line.

- Write every e-mail from work as if your supervisor or other superior at work might read it. E-mail messages written at work are actually owned by your company – meaning that, if they want to, just about anybody in a position of authority can read them. If you write your messages as if they are, you can't get in any trouble.

- Secure your computer with passcodes and other measures so that others can't use your computer terminal without your permission. You may trust your co-workers, but what about vendors who are wandering through the office, service providers who visit to make repairs after hours, or new employees you don't yet know? Make sure you are the only one who uses your computer.

- Let friends know that it's not okay to forward off-color jokes, pornographic video clips, or other inappropriate – or just plain annoying – content to you via e-mail.

And, even if your company does allow a limited amount of personal Internet use and you take advantage of it, some things are off-limits no matter what. These include:

- Job searching. It goes without saying that searching for your next job on company time probably isn't a good idea.

- Pornography or other inappropriate content. If you would be uncomfortable viewing it with your mother, then it doesn't have a place at work, either.

- Gambling or other gaming. Using the Internet to do fairly important personal tasks like checking your bank account balance or e-mailing a child's teacher is okay, but playing games just says that you have nothing better to do or that you don't make work a priority. Work at work. Play at home.

- Illegal downloads. Downloading pirated software or other content is illegal and can put both you and your company at risk.

- Large personal downloads. Downloading a quick song to listen to while at work might be okay; downloading entire movies or album collections that might jam up the server and slow everyone down is not.

A Word on IMing

IMing, or "Instant Messaging," has become a communication staple – especially for those in their twenties or younger. According to recent research, a full 75 percent of Americans 25 and younger use instant messaging on a regular basis.

More and more companies are beginning to encourage or at least accept instant messaging as a means of communicating among employees. However, more than 85 percent of workers who use instant messaging also admit to using the technology for matters completely unrelated to work, like talking with friends, family, or even co-workers, about matters unrelated to work.

Before installing instant messaging software on your work computer, check your company employee manual or handbook to see if they have a policy regarding instant messaging. Because it is a relatively new phenomenon, chances are they won't. Check with a supervisor or trusted co-worker to see if instant messaging is allowed. If it is, limit your instant messaging to communicating with co-workers only, and on work-related matters. Occasional IMing with friends or on non-work-related subjects may be okay, but don't abuse the privilege. And never use instant messaging to discuss risqué, off-color or sensitive matters. Remember, if you would be uncomfortable with your IMing behavior if your supervisor were looking over your shoulder, you've crossed the line.

Written Communication

Not everyone is an Ernest Hemingway, but everyone should know how to write correctly, efficiently and effectively. There are many modes of written communication used in the modern workplace, from quick e-mail messages to more involved business letters, multi-page reports and proposals. Sometimes you will write with the purpose of informing people. Other times you will be trying to persuade someone to take action. There are basic, standard formats for writing all kinds of business documents, but each company has its own style and guidelines. When it is time to write your first memo, or business letter, or report, find a previous example from your company and follow the standards in that example.

Regardless of the kind of document you are writing, however, there are strategies to keep in mind for all business writing. Remember:

- Ask yourself, Who is my audience?
  - Who will read this? What is this reader's background, attitude toward me, and attitude toward my subject matter?
  - What does my reader know about my topic?
  - Who else might end up reading what I write? Could anything be misconstrued by unknown readers and reflect unfavorably on me or the organization?
- Ask yourself, What is the purpose of my message?
  - What action do I want my reader to take after reading my document?
  - What do I want my reader to know or understand?
  - What attitude do I want my reader to have?
- Choose your ideas. Select and list the ideas you need to include to achieve your purpose.
- Put the ideas in order. Arrange your ideas in the most appropriate, most meaningful order.
- Choose a format. Does your subject call for a memo? Or would your audience be better suited for a more formal business letter? Or is the information so extensive that it requires a report?
- Choose a style. Can you be casual and throw in a funny line or two for co-workers? Or is this document for a potential client and therefore in need of a more formal approach?
- Always aim for clarity.

- Avoid wordiness.

- Read your letter aloud to catch ambiguities and errors.

- Revise and rewrite. If necessary, ask a co-worker to read your work and give you feedback.

- Edit. Check spelling, usage, sentence structure, and punctuation.

The Basic Business Letter

While less common in this age of e-mail, voice mail and fax, business letters are still an important tool – and one of the most basic forms of business communication that everyone should be familiar with. You should understand the parts of a business letter and how to write one well.

Business letters should include:

- Date (including month, day and year).

- Sender's Address. Including your address is optional, and shouldn't be typed if the letter is on letterhead that includes your company's address.

- Recipient's Address. Use U.S. Post Office format for addresses.

- Salutation. Use the name on the address to greet the reader. If you know the person and address them by first name, it's fine to use their first name (Dear John:). In all other cases, use the personal title and full name followed by a colon (Dr. John Doe:). Leave one blank line after the salutation.

- Body. The first paragraph should include a friendly opening and the main point of the letter. Subsequent paragraphs should justify the main point and include supporting information and details. The last paragraph should restate the purpose of the letter and, if necessary, request some type of action. Leave a line between each paragraph.

- Closing. Capitalize the first word only ("Thank you" or "Sincerely") and leave four lines between the closing and the sender's signature.

- Enclosures. Indicate any documents enclosed with the letter.

- Typist's Initials. These indicate who typed the letter. If the sender is the typist, omit these initial.

There are various styles of business letters. The two most common styles are the block and indented formats. Examples of these have been provided on the following pages.

Block Format Letter

Life After Graduation, LLC
PO Box 11205
Bainbridge Island, WA 98110

June 19, 2007

Ms. Recent Graduate
Chief Executive Officer, Apex Company
12345 1st Street
Anywhere, USA 56789-1479

Dear Ms. Graduate:

This is the first paragraph of this letter. It should state the purpose of the letter or the reason for writing. This may be the only paragraph that gets read. Therefore, be brief and clear. Write and rewrite until you get it right.

This is the second paragraph of this letter. Most business letters will have more than one paragraph. In addition, the standard business letter will also include some essential elements including the heading, date, address of recipient, salutation, body of text, complimentary closing, handwritten signature, and the name of the sender typed below the signature.

There are, of course, variations of the standard business letter. Be sure to ask your supervisor what, if any, variations you may be required to include in the business letters you write.

I am closing this letter so that I can demonstrate the final elements of a business letter.

Thank you for reading this letter and for reading *Backpack To Briefcase*.

Sincerely,

(signature here)

Terry Arndt
President

mda

Indented Format Letter

Life After Graduation, LLC
PO Box 11205
Bainbridge Island, WA 98110

June 19, 2007

Ms. Recent Graduate
Chief Executive Officer, Apex Company
12345 1st Street
Anywhere, USA 56789-1479

Dear Ms. Graduate:

This is the first paragraph of this letter. It should state the purpose of the letter or the reason for writing. This may be the only paragraph that gets read. Therefore, be brief and clear. Write and rewrite until you get it right.

This is the second paragraph of this letter. Most business letters will have more than one paragraph. In addition, the standard business letter will also include some essential elements including the heading, date, address of recipient, salutation, body of text, complimentary closing, handwritten signature, and the name of the sender typed below the signature.

There are, of course, variations of the standard business letter. Be sure to ask your supervisor what, if any, variations you may be required to include in the business letters you write.

I am closing this letter so that I can demonstrate the final elements of a business letter.

Thank you for reading this letter and for reading *Backpack To Briefcase*.

Sincerely,

(signature here)

Terry Arndt
President

mda

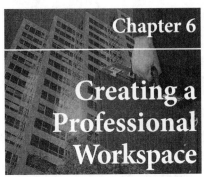

Chapter 6

Creating a Professional Workspace

Though you most likely won't have a corner office with a view this early in your career, you will have some kind of workspace to call your own, whether it's a shared office, a cubicle, a desk or even a corner of a supply closet with a table and chair. The way you decorate and maintain your work area not only affects your efficiency, it is also part of your image.

Organization

Getting and staying organized is one of the best ways to boost your productivity, efficiency – and sanity. A cluttered desk and out-of-control workspace makes things difficult to find and may make people question your ability to handle your job. After all, if you can't create a filing system that works for you, how can your supervisor trust you to handle projects for an important client? Your organizational skills are definitely important to the image you project – and to the work that you produce. Stay organized with these simple recommendations:

- Create a system for organizing immediately that works for you and be disciplined in following it. Decide how you will file, prioritize tasks, and maintain your e-mail and computer files, etc. before things get out of hand.

- If you can't control it, hide it by using attractive containers to contain the clutter. Even if you can only get to your filing once a month, if you keep papers to be filed hidden away in an attractive basket or bin, nobody will be the wiser.

- Try to stick with the "one-touch" rule. Only touch a paper once, then decide what to do with it and take action immediately. Don't put junk mail in a pile – send it straight to the garbage can. If a message is left on your desk, return the call immediately, then throw it away. This method will keep paper clutter to a minimum.

- Studies have shown that office desktops, computer keyboards and phones are some of the dirtiest and germ-filled surfaces we come in contact with. If you eat at your desk regularly, your desk is probably also prone to spills, crumbs and sticky spots. Clean your workspace weekly by removing items and wiping the entire area with a clean, damp cloth.

- Consider investing in a personal organizer – either paper or electronic – to help you maintain organization, scheduling and to-do lists.

- If space is minimal in your work area, be creative. Pocket files can be easily hung on walls to hold often-used files, rolling filing cabinets and storage bins can be stored under desks, and hooks for hanging coats and bags can be hung over doors.

- Keeping your desktop clutter-free, your wastebasket emptied and your bookshelves straight can go a long way toward creating the illusion that you're organized – even if you're still struggling. Spend a few minutes every day straightening and cleaning things to help present an organized image.

- Make sure your organizing system isn't so mysterious that nobody else would ever be able to figure it out. Others might need to be able to find your documents, files and contacts if you should be out sick or away on business or vacation. Label paper files and computer files plainly, and try to keep things where they would logically be kept – books on the bookshelves rather than in desk drawers, contact numbers in the Rolodex on your desk rather than written in a notebook you keep in your purse, documents for clients in the computer file labeled with the client's name, etc.

The Well-Dressed Desk

Of course, you need the standard office supplies – computer, paper, pen, stapler, and so on – and these will most likely be provided to you by your company. However, there are other things you may want to consider keeping in stock in your workplace, for both your comfort and to help you maintain your image at work.

- Healthy, non-perishable snacks to squelch hunger pains while working through the lunch hour or staying late. A few sets of disposable cutlery and some packets of your favorite condiments are great, too, for when the take-out clerk forgot to include them in your order.

- A "first aid" kit with band-aids for paper cuts, antacids for nervous stomachs, and pain relievers for headaches.

- A box of tissues.

- A few personal grooming items for unexpected emergencies, like a toothbrush, dental floss, nail file, a small mirror, etc.

- A travel sewing kit to temporarily fix buttons or small holes in clothing.

- A few stain wipes or a stain stick to treat spills on clothing.

- Some spare clothing – a shirt in case you get a stain before an important meeting, an extra pair of panty hose in case you get a run, etc.

- An umbrella.

- A few dollars and some change for days you can't make it to the bank, for the vending machines and for parking meters when you drive to meetings.

- Instant hand sanitizer to wash your hands without having to go to a sink – great for when you have a cold and want to prevent spreading germs or after you shake hands with someone else who does.

- Antibacterial wipes for cleaning your desk, your phone and your computer keyboard on a regular basis and for mopping up spills.

- A clock, a desk lamp and a calendar.

Home Away From Home

You'll be spending a big part of your life at work so you want to make your workspace personal and comfortable. Make sure you stick to a few guidelines.

- A few pictures in tasteful frames or tacked to your bulletin board are great – just don't go overboard. Ten pictures of you and the person you are dating can make you look like a stalker, and tons of pictures of your niece are just overkill. Keep in mind that the subject of the pictures should also reflect you well. Try to avoid pictures that include you holding alcoholic drinks, wearing revealing clothing, or those that just make you look silly.

- Don't advertise your personal beliefs and values in your cubicle. Overt religious symbols, pin-up calendars, crass sayings tacked to your bulletin board, or your fraternity or sorority paddle nailed to the wall are definite don'ts.

- Your desk or cubicle is not another room in your apartment. Purchasing a stylish desk lamp and one framed picture to hang above your desk is fine; spending hundreds of dollars to make your cubicle look like it was decorated by an interior designer is not. Give your workspace a few touches that express your personal flair, but don't go overboard.

- Consider using a plant to decorate, but make sure you water it. A dead plant doesn't say much for your sense of responsibility.

- Keep in mind that your workspace is most likely shared space – meaning that you have to keep other people's comfort in mind. Your office mate might be allergic to the fresh flowers you like to keep in the vase on your desk, someone that visits your desk on a regular basis for work tasks might hate the way the scented sachet hanging on your bulletin board smells, or the co-worker with a direct view of your candy dish full of fattening treats might be trying to lose weight to improve his/her health. Be mindful of how your space affects others.

- Always remember that even though it's "your" workspace, you are still at work. Office spaces are generally bland for a reason – they're designed for work. Anything in your cubicle that distracts you or others from your main purpose – work – doesn't belong there.

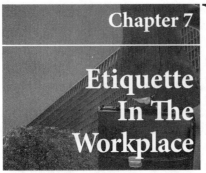

Chapter 7

Etiquette In The Workplace

You don't have to be Ms. Manners to understand that good manners matter – and in the workplace they matter a lot. Being courteous, caring and thoughtful to your colleagues isn't just polite – it's good for your career. And while mom might have taught most of us the basics (don't talk with your mouth full, say please and thank you, don't leave the front door open), workplace etiquette can be a little more complex. Not to worry, however. With a little thought, even the trickiest of workplace manners can be mastered.

Using Office Resources

Working in an office means working with a lot of shared resources, including fax machines, copiers, telephone systems, printers, and the office supply closet. Every office has different protocols regarding shared resources – some, for example, have entire IT departments to handle maintenance and repairs on all computer systems and accessories, while others call repair services only as needed – and you should make yourself familiar with these protocols as soon as possible. During your first week at your new job, ask someone to demonstrate how to use all office machines and the best ways to access resources. Also, find out to whom you should report low supplies, repair or maintenance needs and problems. Some other things to keep in mind:

- Leave it like you found it. Leave paper trays full, work areas neat, supplies on the right shelf, and fax machines cleared of all numbers.

- Take initiative to address problems as they come up. If you notice the "Low Toner" light is blinking while using the copier, don't ignore it – replace it. It may take a few extra minutes and a little bit of hassle – but you'll be happy you did it when someone does the same for you.

- Don't hoard resources. You might be tempted to store 10 legal pads and 20 of your favorite pens in your desk drawer "just in case," but others need those items as well. And just because you use the paper cutter on a fairly regular basis doesn't mean that it belongs on your desk instead of in the supply closet where it is supposed to be, and where others who need it can find it.

- If you break it, own up to it. If you jam the copier, short out the fax machine, or topple a stack of office supplies in the closet, admit it – then try to remedy the situation. If it's beyond your capabilities – the copy repair service needs to be called, for example – let the proper person know about the problem so it can be addressed immediately.

- Become friends with owner's manuals. Copiers, fax machines, printers and the like are notorious for eating paper, jamming and generally causing problems. However, most problems are easily remedied by following directions outlined in the owner's manuals. Don't think that passing by the receptionist's desk or the IT department and mentioning that the color copier is blinking an error message is doing your part. If a problem is minor and can be fixed by a few minutes of effort on your part, then do it.

- Use the fair warning system. If you know you are about to receive a 40-page fax, or need to print a 200-page document on the shared printer, let everyone know so they can plan around it. If you're making hundreds of copies but Amanda from accounting needs to make only one, take a break from your job to let her cut in and make her copy. It may be a pain to interrupt your flow, but it's better than being considered a pain.

Your Mother Doesn't Work Here

It's a common occurrence in office life: the note tacked to the break room bulletin board or stuck to the communal fridge by a well-meaning office manager, receptionist or other poor employee usually delegated the job of cleaning up after those who don't clean up after themselves. "*YOUR MOTHER DOESN'T WORK HERE. KINDLY CLEAN UP AFTER YOURSELF.*" Just a friendly reminder, usually after a six-month-old Tupperware container growing mold was unearthed in the fridge, or coffee grinds were cleaned out of the sink for the tenth time that week, or dishes were left, unwashed, in the sink for days. It seems like common sense to clean up after yourself at the office, but when days are busy and distractions are many, it can be easy to let some things slide – especially when someone else will probably pick up the slack. Make sure you're not the office slob by remembering a few simple rules and tips:

- During your first week of work, find out the rules of the communal spaces. For example, is coffee there for everyone, or only for those who pitch into a monthly "coffee club"? Who makes the coffee – the first one in the door, or the office receptionist? Are the dishes and mugs in the cabinets for communal use or do you need to bring your own? Do you empty your own wastebasket into a larger trashcan or dumpster, or does a custodian take care of it? Does the office recycle paper, cans, and newspapers? Making yourself familiar with office policies will go a long way toward helping you avoid making a faux pas.

- If you mess it up, clean it up – this includes all communal spaces like kitchens, break rooms, bathrooms, meeting rooms, reception areas, as well as parking lots and outdoor eating areas.

- Wash your dishes and clean up your messes immediately. You may think that you'll do it later, but you may forget during the busy day. Also, while your messes are waiting for "later," your co-workers are noticing the mess and trying to figure out who left it.

- If you use the last of something – toilet paper, coffee filters, paper towels, etc. – replace it. If the stock room is out of a supply or running low, let the proper person know.

- Cover your food with a plate or paper towel when using the communal microwave. It's easier to avoid splatters and spills than to clean them up. And, there's nothing worse than going to use the microwave and finding that it's covered with baked-on spaghetti sauce!

- Leave no trace. If you bring a lunch in the morning, remember to bring what ever is left at the end of the day home with you. Don't leave it in the fridge for "later."

- Make sure your food is tightly covered. Nobody wants to smell your lunch, or worse, discover that his or her lunch has started to taste like your lunch after sharing space in the fridge.

- Most office environments have a trash service that only empties trash every other day or, possibly, only once a week. Don't use your office wastebasket or communal trash cans to dispose of potentially smelly or unusually messy waste. Instead, empty soda cans completely before throwing them in wastebaskets, take food items that spoil straight to the dumpster, and dispose of your used tissues in the bathroom when you have a cold.

- Keep in mind that someone cleans the bathroom, vacuums, polishes the furniture, and washes the windows, and his/her job is difficult enough already. If you make an out-of-the-ordinary mess on the floor while shredding documents, spill an entire container of soap on the bathroom floor, or leave sticky marks on the conference table, do your best to clean it up, or, at the very least, apologize and let the proper person know what has happened so it won't be an unpleasant surprise.

- Pay attention to the general cleanliness and tidiness of the office, especially if it is considered everybody's job to keep the workplace in order. If filing is piling up, furniture needs to be dusted, or clutter needs to be controlled, take the initiative to pitch in. People notice when you do nice things – and notice even more when you never do.

Living the Cubicle Life

Everyone dreams of that corner office with a view; it's practically part of the American Dream. But, most likely, your first office will be housed in that staple of modern office life – the cubicle.

Many offices use a system of dividers to section off work areas, or "cubicles." Other offices have an open floor plan with desks arranged into "pods." You will probably be sharing an office with one or more people and might even be relegated to a corner in a communal area like the copy room until a better office space can be found. Working like this can sometimes feel like living in a goldfish bowl, and the irritations of sharing space are quickly apparent. Make cubicle life easier – for everyone – by keeping in mind a few tried and true rules:

- Noise travels. When working in close quarters, noise is part of the deal. But don't contribute more than your share. While in the office keep your cell phone on vibrate or turn it off. Use the speakerphone only when absolutely necessary. If you are allowed to play music while working, keep it at a volume that only you can hear. Keep in mind that your voice projects – not everyone wants to hear the details of every one of your phone conversations. And forego the convenience of e-mail alerts for the sanity of your co-workers.

- Smells aren't all good. Not everyone loves the smell of your broccoli-casserole lunch or your latest potpourri selection. Enjoy foods with strong odors at home. That goes for scented candles, potpourri, air fresheners, and strong perfumes and colognes as well. What might be a pleasant aroma to you could trigger an allergic reaction for a co-worker.

- Keep personal things personal. Nobody wants to hear you fight with your mother on the phone or gossip with your favorite co-worker. Always remember that the partition of your cubicle or the thin walls of your shared office offer limited privacy. Assume that everyone can hear everything and act accordingly.

- Repeat nothing of what you hear or see. Working in small spaces means that occasionally you'll probably hear or see more than you want to. Keep in mind that you don't have to let everyone else know that you overheard your co-worker fighting with creditors or saw him straightening his toupee. Things aren't always what they seem – and the office gossip isn't a position to aspire to.

- Keep it neat. Working in cubicles or other shared spaces means you need to do you part to keep your workspace reasonably clean, organized and clutter-free.

- Program your office phone to ring at an appropriate noise level. In addition, program your voice mail to pick up after just a couple rings.

- Meeting rooms are for meetings. Brainstorming for a project is best done behind closed doors, where it won't bother anybody else. It may be easier to squeeze everyone into your cubicle than reserving space and time in a meeting room, but your co-workers will appreciate it if you make the effort to preserve their quiet.

- Knock before entering. It may seem silly to knock on a cubicle when there's no door, but it's only good manners to ask someone if it's a good time before you interrupt.

Taking a Break

Sometimes you just need a break. Review your office policies regarding breaks. Do you get a paid lunch break? Is it one hour or one half hour? Are you allowed additional breaks throughout the day? Some offices don't formally outline their break policies, but instead rely on their employees to use good judgment. If this is the case with your employer, ask a fellow employee how breaks are generally handled, and spend some time observing others' behavior.

The Lunch Break

Of course, everyone needs to eat, and the lunch break is a given at nearly all businesses. However, every workplace has different rules and protocols regarding lunch breaks.

Some office buildings have cafeterias or delis in the lobbies and employees are expected to take their lunch breaks there, where they are available if needed and don't have to leave the premises for long periods of time. Other offices make a habit of taking group orders and ordering food in on a daily basis. You may find that your office mates make a habit of bringing their lunch from home every day and eating at their desk. Or, you may find that lunch breaks are a social occasion, where groups of people from the office head to the latest eatery for an hour of eating and hanging out. Your office may even have a great break room that's fully equipped for cooking and storing food and where everyone eats at different times throughout the day.

Also remember that because eating is something of a social occasion, the lunch hour can be important to your work relationships. If everyone in your department always goes out together for lunch, but you decline their invitation every day, you may be branded as anti-social. On the other hand, if you and a few of your co-workers make a habit of going to lunch together every Wednesday but don't extend invitations to others in the office, it may result in hurt feelings or accusations that you are forming a clique. Be mindful of how your actions affect others.

The 15-Minute Break

Eight or more hours makes for a long day – and sometimes one lunch break just doesn't cut it. That's where the more elusive 10- or 15-minute break comes in. You won't hear a bell going off indicating that it's time to take your scheduled mid-morning break, but taking one or two short breaks a day is usually fine in most office environments.

Taking a few minutes respite from a tedious project to go outside to enjoy a nice day can be great for productivity by renewing your energy and enthusiasm for work. Many productivity experts even suggest taking a minute or two every hour to get up from your desk, do a few stretches, laugh with a co-worker, or just walk to get a drink of water. Make sure you use these breaks wisely and that your supervisor agrees they are important.

The Smoking Break

More problematic these days is the smoking break. Once commonplace in working life, the smoking break used to be a time for co-workers to commiserate and relax from the stress of the workday. However, smoking is now considered a bad habit and is discouraged in most workplaces.

If you have a smoking habit, you must be sure to handle it with courtesy and discretion. Find out where you are allowed to smoke in the perimeter of the office building. Some buildings have special smoking "tents" or awnings where employees are allowed to smoke. Others require that smokers be at least 25 feet from the building. Be sure not to litter the front of your office building with discarded butts; most buildings will provide a receptacle in which you can dispose of them. Keep your smoking breaks to a minimum; let someone know where you will be and when you will be back, and try your best not to let the smell of smoke follow you back into the office.

Most importantly, don't use your bad habit as an excuse to abuse your employer's break policy. Non-smokers will resent that you are taking extra time off and it won't win you any points with management, either.

The Annoying Co-Worker

Chews with his mouth open. Laughs like a hyena at just about everything. Complains to anyone who will listen. Sound familiar? Every office has at least one annoying co-worker, and irritating each other is just inevitable in a work environment. And it's more than just bothersome. In fact, One Gallup Poll found that negativity among workers due to annoying behaviors costs the U.S. $300 billion a year in lost productivity. Don't become the office annoyance. Here's an outline of the most annoying behaviors at work:

- Interrupting people while they are working, talking, or in the middle of something important.

- Talking loudly while on the phone, slamming doors, having loud conversations, clearing your throat loudly and regularly – basically making any loud and distracting noises on a regular basis.

- Faking helplessness to get out of doing work. Nothing's worse than the person who can't – or won't – learn how to do simple tasks (like fixing copier paper jams, for example) because they know that someone else will do them instead.

- Coming to work when you are sick and spreading your germs. People think they are showing their dedication when they stick out a day at work while battling the flu, but nothing could be farther from the truth. Going to work ill and getting everyone else sick doesn't help anyone or prove anything.

- Selling stuff at work – Avon, Amway, your kid's school fundraiser items. Nobody wants to be pressured to buy something they don't want at the workplace.

- Doing stuff at work that you should be doing at home. This includes downloading music, making calls to plan your wedding, shopping online for gifts and even more personal activities like flossing or painting your nails. Believe it or not, people actually do these things!

- Being chronically late, unprepared, unorganized and full of excuses.

- Sharing detailed information about your life – the fight you had this morning with your boyfriend, the weird dream you had about your third-grade teacher last night – with everyone, despite whether they are interested or not.

- Making the rounds and telling the same funny story, so that every person in the office has to hear it 14 times.

- Borrowing stuff and not returning it.

- Complaining rather than working proactively to address problems or make changes.

So what to do about it? First of all, make sure you aren't the culprit. Second, try to ignore it. Everyone is annoying at least once in a while, and modern life has given us all shorter fuses. Everybody deserves at least one shot at redemption, so don't be too quick to judge. However, if annoying behaviors go beyond just annoying and start to affect productivity or workplace morale, they must be addressed. A first line of defense is to just to be honest and let the person know that what he/she is doing is, well, annoying. If that doesn't remedy the situation, it's best to take it up with a supervisor or the human resources department.

Office Politics

Office politics: every workplace has its share, and it's not all bad. In fact, in order to achieve career success, you must learn to master a certain amount of office politics. Here's how.

By definition, politics is dealing with people in a way that produces outcomes that are beneficial to you. Nothing wrong with that, right? Right – as long as the playing field is even and people conduct themselves with integrity. Unfortunately, this isn't always the case. The bad news is that in your work life you will come across people who brown nose, lie, take credit for work they didn't do, and other generally unsavory characters. The good news is that most people are good, fair people who want the same things that you do: to earn a living while learning and growing as a person, being recognized for a job well done, helping others and having a little fun along the way.

The best news is that to become a pro at office politicking, you don't have to do much more than be a good person. Take a look at the following tips for achieving success in office politics:

- Develop a genuine interest in other people. If you are really interested in other people's experiences, opinions and perspectives, demonstrate caring, team spirit, and a willingness to open yourself up to other ways of thinking. All of these traits will help you get ahead – plus it's just a more interesting and fulfilling way to live!

- Develop a healthy curiosity about the world. Curiosity about how the world works leads to growth, learning and a more well-rounded experience, all great things to have when it comes to getting ahead at the office.

- Be empathetic. Half of being a successful office "politician" is understanding what other people want and need.

- Be a good listener. It's hard to empathize with people or express your interest in who they are if you aren't even listening to what they say. Developing good listening skills is key to playing the office politics game.

- Make time for other people. You might think that keeping your head down and putting your nose to the grindstone is the best way to get ahead at work, but you're missing half of the picture. While hard work is appreciated and rewarded, you also have to be likeable and interesting, demonstrate good character, and show that you care about other people in order to achieve career success. All of this is hard to do if you don't take the time to get to know your colleagues – and, yes, participate in a little office politics.

- Be true to yourself. If, in the course of office politics, you begin to feel fake or dishonest, you're going about it the wrong way. You shouldn't have to be someone else to be successful in office politics – you should only have to be your best self.

- Develop gratitude. Being truly grateful for your job, the people who have helped you, and all the positive things in your life is a great way to develop a positive, can-do attitude. Take the time every day to think about what you are grateful for.

- Be positive, respectful and considerate. Act like the person you want to work with.

Office Politics Pitfalls

As essential as it is, office politics isn't always pretty. The truth is it can be downright ugly, but don't think that you have to lower yourself to the lowest common denominator. As comedienne Lily Tomlin famously said, "The problem with the rat race is that even if you win, you're still a rat." By recognizing the most common office politics pitfalls and employing some simple strategies to avoid them, you can sidestep problems and keep your career on track.

Cliques

It's human nature – people with similar interests or experience tend to group together. It's no different at work – the younger single women tend to become work buddies, people who enjoy computers seek each other out in the workplace, working mothers will take their lunch breaks together to discuss kids. There's nothing wrong with developing groups of friends at the office, until it leads to the exclusion of others, hurt feelings and bad morale.

Make sure you're not guilty of creating an office clique by being mindful of others' feelings. Invite co-workers to join you and your friends for lunch, make sure that everyone is always in on the conversation and the joke, and don't give anyone special treatment at the office just because they are your friend. And if you find that you are on the outside of an office clique, don't sweat it. Do your best to be friendly, courteous and helpful to everyone you work with, and work friendships and alliances will develop naturally and fairly.

Gossip

Unfortunately, gossip is all but unavoidable in the workplace. The office "grapevine" is a staple of modern office life, and does serve its purpose. If not wildly speculative, malicious, or untrue, gossip can be a relatively harmless way to bond with co-workers and spread fun and positive news. For example, telling your office mate that Sheila from the IT department got engaged over the weekend and looks really happy is, by most definitions, gossip. But it's also harmless. On the other hand, repeating that you heard Shelia's getting divorced because her husband cheated on her with his secretary isn't harmless – it's hurtful. At its worst, gossip can hurt feelings, lower morale, and even damage or destroy careers. And you don't have to be the subject of gossip to be harmed by it: earning a reputation as an office gossip means you appear disloyal, untrustworthy, superficial, or dishonest in the eyes of colleagues and supervisors.

The best way to figure out if you are repeating harmless news or spreading potentially hurtful gossip is to evaluate your motivation behind repeating it. If your motive is to promote yourself, get attention, or to be the center of attention, you are gossiping. Ask yourself this: How would the subject of this news feel if he or she heard me repeating the news. To be truly gossip-free, you have to stop gossip in its tracks – and refuse to listen to it too. If someone starts repeating gossip to you, simply stop them and let them know that you are uncomfortable with the subject matter.

Favoritism, back stabbing, sabotage and other nasty office behavior

It's inevitable – from time to time you will encounter people in your career who are dishonest, unfair, unscrupulous or just plain mean. We all want to consider our co-workers friends, but what to do if you become the object of a co-worker's dirty politics? You don't have to just take it if you are being affected by favoritism, co-worker sabotage, gossip or backstabbing. By using a few simple strategies, you can rise above the drama and stay on course.

- **Develop a Paper Trail as a Precaution** – Always keep meticulous records of your office communications and work. That way, if a co-worker tries to accuse you of falling behind on work, or a supervisor unfairly claims to have passed you over for a prime assignment because the quality of your work is poor, you can respond with confidence by using your arsenal of proof to the contrary.

- **Don't Suffer in Silence** – The squeaky wheel gets the grease. If colleagues are unfairly trying to undermine your career or one-up you, making your accomplishments and value known is a great counter-strategy. Make sure your boss knows about your successes and strengths.

- **Take the High Road** – It's never a good policy to roll in the mud with your enemies. If you are the target of dirty office politics, rise above it by staying calm, focusing on the positive, and proactively – and fairly – addressing the problem. Don't let what is going on affect your job performance or your confidence – that's exactly what the saboteur wants.

- **Learn to Communicate** – Sometimes, simple communication is the answer. Speaking calmly and directly to the person who is at the root of the problem can go a long way to solving personality conflicts. Honest and open communication can help you understand your co-worker's perspective, and may even make your co-worker aware of how his behavior is affecting you.

Chapter 8

Tips For Business-Related Functions

Work isn't just about sitting behind a desk with your nose to the grindstone. In fact, in your career you will encounter a variety of business functions that will take you outside of the office. The way you conduct yourself during these functions is just as important – and sometimes more important – than the way you conduct yourself during the standard work day. Handle business functions with class, finesse and professionalism and you will surely move up the ladder of success. Here's how.

Business Meetings

Meetings are the most common way for groups to make decisions, solve problems, educate people, and plan programs and projects. At their best, meetings can be productive and accomplish goals, but at their worst they can be frustrating and squash enthusiasm. According to a study by the Wharton Center for Applied Research, some U.S. workers spend as much as 23 hours a week in meetings. What's more, most managers say that only 56 percent of meetings are productive! Don't be a victim – or worse, a perpetrator – of the bad meeting. Get the most out of meetings by following these tips:

If you are leading the meeting:

- Planning equals productivity. Set an agenda and send it to everyone who will attend the meeting ahead of time. Consult with meeting participants to see if there are items they would like to add to the agenda. If meeting participants will be called upon to provide feedback during the meeting, be sure to note that in the agenda and be sure to provide the participants any necessary information they may need to prepare for the meeting.

- Notify people about the meeting early so they can plan accordingly and won't be annoyed that their day has been interrupted.

- Make sure the meeting room is big enough to accommodate everyone and that there is enough seating.

- If the meeting is large and not everyone will know each other, consider using nametags.

- Start and end the meeting on time – it shows respect for other people's time and ensures that everyone will be able to attend the entire meeting.

- Begin by making necessary introductions, then by summarizing the purpose of the meeting and the points to be covered.

- Encourage participation from everyone.

- Consider creating some ground rules for the meeting, including:

    - Everyone has equal rights and can participate.

    - The will of the majority is carried out.

    - The minority will be heard.

    - Only one topic will be considered at a time.

    - Decision-making will be done fairly and impartially.

- Know how decisions will be made ahead of time. A democratic vote? By committee?

- Use visual aids – a chalkboard, a slideshow, a flipchart, etc.

- Stay focused and on topic.

- Have a game plan for dealing with conflict.

- Create an "action sheet" for the meeting to distribute to everyone as a follow up. This action sheet should include a brief summary of the meeting, agreed-upon items for further action, and the time, date and location of the next meeting, if there is to be one.

- Afterward, evaluate the success of the meeting and ask for others' input. This will help you to run an even better meeting the next time around.

If you are participating in a meeting:

- Let those running the meeting know if you will attend as soon as possible.

- Be on time.

- Be prepared by bringing all necessary materials, gathering and organizing your thoughts and reviewing the agenda ahead of time.

- Stay on topic and don't bring up irrelevant points or subjects that will cause the discussion to drift.

- Don't interrupt.
- Participate. Avoid looking like you are filling space. Show interest and involvement in the discussion by making comments and asking questions.
- Take notes.
- Don't be critical or negative.
- If asked, give the meeting leader constructive input on what went well and how the meeting could have been even better.
- Summarize your notes and offer to share with other meeting participants to ensure that everyone is on the same page.

Business Meals

Everyone likes to eat, so it's no surprise that meals are a big part of doing business. Many a deal has been closed over dinner and drinks, and business meals are a common way to entertain clients, develop professional relationships, or conduct meetings in a more social environment. The way you conduct yourself during these meals is important, so you'll want to keep the following rules and strategies in mind.

Types of Business Meals
Business can be conducted during just about any kind of meal at restaurants, at someone's home or in the conference room, in a casual or formal environment, and may be impromptu or scheduled.

Breakfast Meetings: Breakfast meetings often take place before the work day begins and might be scheduled to brainstorm or set the agenda for the day, or to fit in a meeting in an otherwise packed schedule. You may meet at a restaurant, or bagels and coffee might be ordered in to the office conference room. Breakfast meetings are normally casual and brief, and last no longer than 90 minutes.

Lunch Meetings: Lunch meetings are commonly used for networking (hence the cliché – "Let's do lunch"), meeting with clients, or for in-depth discussions about work matters. They often take place in restaurants, but you will also find that companies sometimes schedule working lunches during crunch times. Lunch meetings range from very casual (meeting for lunch with a few colleagues to discuss strategies for an upcoming project, for example) to more formal (meeting for the first time at a nice restaurant with a potential client). Lunch meetings can last longer than breakfast meetings, but because most participants normally need to return to work, these meals typically don't run longer than two hours.

Dinner Meetings: Dinner meetings are normally the most formal of business meals, lasting up to three hours and nearly always held at a restaurant. Because they typically take place outside of the work day, they are usually scheduled well in advance. Dinner meetings are most commonly used to entertain clients or potential clients, to network, or to celebrate with colleagues.

As the Host

As the host, it is your responsibility to ensure that the business meal goes well and that the necessary business is conducted. Make sure you are prepared, organized and polished by keeping the following in mind:

- Preparation is key to a successful business meal. Think carefully about the meeting time, place and agenda; give guests plenty of notice so they can fit the meeting into their schedule.

- Let guests know in advance what business will be conducted at the meal so they can be prepared as well.

- Always make reservations in advance and confirm the reservations a day before the event. Choose a restaurant that you are confident will provide good service, good food and offer a menu that will satisfy everyone. If you are unfamiliar with area restaurants, ask someone you trust for recommendations.

- Arrive at the restaurant early so that you can communicate with restaurant staff, arrange for payment of the bill, make sure the table is appropriate, and greet guests.

- Do not order until all the guests have arrived.

- If you must be late, contact the restaurant to let them know that your guests should be seated and offered drinks and appetizers until you arrive. Try to contact your guests as well to apologize for your delay and let them know that they should go ahead and be seated and begin their order.

- Allow your guests to choose their place at the table, and offer them the preferred seating, such as the seat with the view of the window or at the head of the table.

- Always allow your guests to order first.

- If you have not arranged for payment ahead of time, arrange for the bill to be delivered to you at the end of the meal. Always pay for business meals that you have hosted.

- Thank your guests for attending.

- Tip the servers well (20-percent is standard) and thank the restaurant manager if the service was exceptional. A good restaurant and restaurant staff that you can rely on to support your important business meals is a great asset.

- If necessary, follow up business meals with an e-mail, memo or call to summarize the business that was conducted during the meal and remind attendees of action items.

As the Guest

Make your host's job as easy as possible by remembering the following tips:

- Be sure to RSVP for any business meal as soon as possible.

- Be sure you understand the reason for the business meal and know what matters will be discussed.

- If you have special dietary needs, let the host know. For example, if you have a seafood allergy, your host will want to know that so he doesn't schedule the meeting at a seafood restaurant.

- Come to the business meal the way you would to any meeting – prepared and organized.

- Arrive on time or a little early. If you must be late, try to contact your host. At the very least, contact the restaurant to have a staff member pass on a message to your host that you will be late.

- Wait to sit at the table until your host indicates that you should be seated.

- Avoid ordering the most expensive item on the menu.

- If the bill for the meal is placed in front of you by accident, wait for the host to correct the mistake. If the host does not make an attempt to correct the mistake, offer to split the expense. Always come prepared to split the expense for the meal.

- Always thank your host for his/her hospitality.

Dining Etiquette

No doubt you have eaten in countless restaurants before and are familiar with meal etiquette. However, it always pays to review your etiquette know-how before an important business meal. Remember:

- During the meal, keep your cell phone off or program it to vibrate.

- Wait to pick up the menu until the host picks up his.

- Immediately after being seated, remove your napkin from the table, unfold it and place it in your lap.

- Never crumple your napkin, shake it out, or stuff it in your clothing.

- If your napkin falls on the floor, don't pick it up. Instead, ask your server for a new one.

- If you get up during the meal, place your napkin on your chair, not on the table.

- Make sure you fully understand how your food will be prepared and what ingredients are included so you do not order something you are unable to enjoy. If you are unsure, ask the server.

- Avoid ordering messy foods that are difficult to eat gracefully, such as long pastas or shellfish. Also avoid ordering foods you are unfamiliar with as you may not know the proper way to handle and eat them.

- Do not rest your elbows or arms on the table while eating.

- Excuse yourself to the restroom if you must apply cosmetics or take medicine.

- Do not send food back unless it is inedible. If you must send food back, be as discreet and polite as possible.

- Never place used utensils on the table or tablecloth. Instead rest them on the edge of your plate. The knife should rest on the back edge, while the fork and spoon should rest on the sides.

- Bring your food to your mouth, not your mouth to the food.

- Never blow on your food to cool it off.

- Chew with your mouth closed and never speak with your mouth full of food.

- Do not "double dip" in communal foods, such as appetizer dips.

- Do not scrape your plate.

- Only use your hands to handle food when appropriate – when eating sandwiches or berries, for example. If food falls off your plate onto the table, pick it up with your utensils and place it on the edge of your plate.

- Never pick up items that fall onto the floor. Instead, ask for assistance from your server.

- When eating soup, place your spoon into the soup along the bowl edge closest to you. Move the spoon toward the opposite edge until it is about two-thirds full. Lift the spoon from the bowl and rub the bottom of the spoon on the inside edge to avoid any drips. Sip the soup from the spoon – never slurp it. Never lift your soup bowl. To retrieve the soup from the bottom of the bowl, tip the bowl away from you slightly.

- Never hold a knife in your hand while eating. You should cut enough food for one or two bites at a time, place the knife on the top rim of your plate, then eat the pieces you have prepared.

- Try to eat at the same pace as the other guests.

- If you suspect that you have food in your teeth, excuse yourself and attend to it in the restroom, not at the table.

- To inform your server that you have finished your meal, lay your fork and knife next to each other diagonally across your plate (from the 4 o'clock to 11 o'clock position with the sharp edge of the knife facing away from you.

- After finishing your meal, place your napkin to the left of your plate, unfolded.

The Place Setting

The place setting for a meal can be intimidating. However, remembering a few basic points will make you a formal dining pro. A diagram of a semi-formal place setting has been provided at the end of this section for your review.

- A simple way to remember the layout of a place setting is that all utensils to the right of the plate (besides the knife) are for drinking. All the utensils to the left of the plate are for eating.

- If you are ever unsure of what utensil to use when eating or drinking, wait for your host or other guests to begin and then follow their lead.

- As you begin your meal, use the outermost fork or spoon first and work your way in towards the service plate with each course.

- Never place used utensils on the table or tablecloth. Instead, place them on the outer edge of your plate. The knife should rest on the back edge of the plate and the fork and spoon should rest on the sides. When preparing coffee or tea, place the teaspoon on the saucer.

- Depending on the restaurant, the dessert utensils may or may not be present during the initial part of the meal. In some cases, these utensils are only presented once dessert has been ordered. However, in a formal situation, or when a prearranged meal is being served, guests are aware that dessert will be served by the placement of a dessert fork and spoon located horizontally above the plate. Before dessert is served, the server will clear any remaining utensils and food from your dining area and move the dessert fork and spoon into their appropriate position.

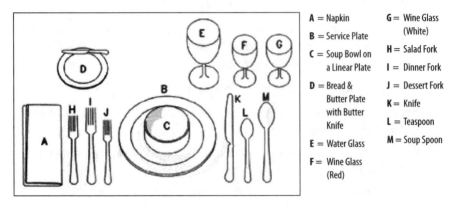

A = Napkin

B = Service Plate

C = Soup Bowl on a Linear Plate

D = Bread & Butter Plate with Butter Knife

E = Water Glass

F = Wine Glass (Red)

G = Wine Glass (White)

H = Salad Fork

I = Dinner Fork

J = Dessert Fork

K = Knife

L = Teaspoon

M = Soup Spoon

Other Important Dining Tips to Remember

So, you've got your etiquette down. You're prepared and organized and ready to work and dine. Wait – there are a few more important tips:

- Be sure to review your company's policies regarding the use of alcohol during business functions, and make sure you follow them. If your company does not have a policy, consult your supervisor.

- If your host asks if you would like a cocktail and you are not sure if anyone else will be ordering one, request water or soda. You can always order a cocktail later.

- Never feel obliged to order alcohol or to explain yourself if you abstain.

- Know your limits when it comes to alcohol and stick to them! A few drinks are not worth losing your job or compromising your credibility or integrity with your colleagues and supervisors.

- Conversation is important at a business meal – try to be outgoing and engaging.

- Delay discussing business until everyone has ordered so that everyone can participate and direct his/her full attention to the business at hand.

- Complete the meal before presenting any documents.

- A restaurant is not an ideal location to discuss sensitive business subjects – you never know who is within earshot.

- Always treat restaurant staff with respect; the way you treat those who serve you is often a good indication of your character.

- If you are unsure of meal etiquette or have little confidence in your ability to conduct yourself properly during meals, buy an etiquette book or even consider taking a class at a local finishing school, which usually offer adult classes for just that reason!

Staff Retreats

Staff retreats are gatherings in a relaxed setting with the goal of sharing ideas, reflecting on experiences, discussing business issues, learning new skills, setting agendas and action plans, and working on team building. Retreats can be as simple as a day-long event at a local conference center, or as elaborate as a week-long, vacation-like event at a resort destination. Staff retreats are supposed to be learning experiences. Make the most of it by remembering the following tips:

- Be prepared. Know what will be discussed and what will be expected of you ahead of time so you can prepare yourself and organize materials.

- View the retreat as an opportunity. Keep a positive attitude about the retreat and view it for what it is – an opportunity to get to know your co-workers better, grow as an employee, and learn about your organization's goals, mission and future.

- Participate! Your organization's leadership has planned the retreat because they want it to be productive and they believe it will be helpful. No matter how silly the activity may seem, it can't hurt to participate. You may learn something new, build a better relationship with a colleague or supervisor, or get an important issue out into the open.

- While staff retreats are often times to communicate honestly and openly, they are not gripe sessions. Avoid complaining and try to remain positive and proactive.

Office Parties

It's the stuff that urban legend is made of – the office Christmas party. You've heard the lampshade-on-the head and body-parts on the copy-machine stories. They're good for a laugh – until you are the one they're laughing at. Throughout your career, you will be invited – or perhaps even required – to attend a range of office celebrations from holiday parties and summer picnics to award ceremonies and retirement parties.

Make sure you don't become the stuff of office lore by following these recommendations for office celebrations.

- Remember that although office parties are social events, they are still business events, too. Behave professionally and as if you are being observed every minute.
- Attend, if only for a while. Turning down invitations to business social functions can make you appear ungrateful or anti-social.
- Spend at least 30 minutes at the party but don't overstay your welcome by partying until the early morning hours.
- Dress appropriately. Skip anything revealing, gimmicky or flashy.
- Don't spend the entire time talking business – you'll be considered boring.
- Avoid controversial subjects, such as religion, politics, and off-color jokes. Don't use the time to complain or gossip either.
- Keep your drink in your left hand, so you are not offering people a cold, wet handshake.
- Keep drinking in check. Moderation is key.
- Use the time to network and build or strengthen relationships with people you may not see regularly, such as top management, people from other departments, and employees from other locations. Don't spend the whole time talking with your office mate or best friend.
- Feel free to dance if its part of the festivities, but keep it tasteful.
- Remember that friends or significant others are not always on the guest list for office parties. If guests are permitted, make sure you bring one who will represent you well.
- Remember to thank the person responsible for planning and coordinating the party. Sending a thank-you note to top management for hosting the party is a nice touch as well.
- Don't drink and drive – or let co-workers drink and drive either. If you believe a co-worker is too compromised to drive home, offer to call a cab or drive him/her home.

Social Events Outside the Office

You will, from time to time, be with supervisors and colleagues in social settings beyond the office walls. Some examples of this might include:

- Playing golf, racquetball or another sport with colleagues.

- Attending the same church as a colleague.

- Joining the same club, professional association or hobby circle as a co-worker.

- Seeing co-workers around town – in restaurants, bars, theaters, shopping centers, grocery stores or gyms.

- Taking classes at the local community center or college with a co-worker.

- Being invited to work friends' weddings, showers, birthday celebrations and holiday parties.

Whether these meetings are planned or by chance, the way you conduct yourself during these times is important to co-workers' perceptions of you. However, while being invited to a golf outing by a supervisor can be a boon to your career, running into the company CEO after you have had too much to drink can be disastrous. To be prepared for these situations, remember:

- Never pretend that you don't see the other person, no matter how much you might want to. Chances are he or she will notice and be angry, hurt or both.

- When greeting your colleague, introduce yourself immediately by name – it's easy for people to have problems recognizing others out of context or on the spur of the moment. Don't be upset or embarrassed if a colleague doesn't remember your name or doesn't seem to recognize you at first – just realize that he/she was taken by surprise.

- Always introduce everyone in your party to your colleague.

- If you have had too much to drink or are in the company of a friend or family member who you fear might say too much or do something unbecoming, greet your colleague, be friendly, but excuse yourself as quickly as possible.

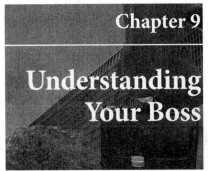

Chapter 9

Understanding Your Boss

One of the most important relationships you will have at work is the one you develop with your boss. Research shows that employees who get along with their bosses are more productive, experience less stress, and are more satisfied with their careers. Your boss can be an asset to your career, a real supporter and a key to your success. On the other hand, your boss can be your biggest detractor and a detriment to your career.

Relationships with bosses are like any relationship: they require mutual respect, communication, compromise, honesty and work to develop and maintain over time. Some bosses can be easier to get along with than others. And some can be downright impossible to work with.

You can't control what kind of boss you have, and you can't change your boss's behavior or personality. To ensure that you are doing everything you can to develop a healthy relationship with the person who may play a leading role in your career, implement these key strategies:

- **Show Respect** – It's reasonable to assume that your boss is the boss because she earned it. Therefore she deserves your respect – and will return your efforts by respecting you as well.

- **Give Your Best** – If you give your best effort, what else can your boss ask for?

- **Be Honest** – If your boss asks for feedback, give it to her. If there's a problem, admit it. And if you make a mistake, own up to it as soon as you can.

- **Give Your Boss Fair Notice** – If you want to plan a vacation, need time off for illness, or may experience problems being on time due to family responsibilities, let your boss know. She may be very understanding, and at the very least will appreciate your candor so that she can make plans for your absence. This goes for your resignation as well. Even though your boss may not be your boss for long, she may be willing to serve as a useful reference or mentor. Give her fair advance notice of your departure to keep the relationship friendly.

- **Maintain Boundaries** – You want to have a great relationship with your boss, but you don't have to be best friends. Don't share very personal information – your boss doesn't need to know the details of your latest romantic relationship or how you spend every minute of your off time. And keep in mind that your boss is still your boss, no matter how strong your relationship is – and she may have to make unpopular or difficult decisions.

- **Be Positive** – Nobody likes a complainer – especially the boss. Communicate with questions, not complaints.

- **Manage Your Emotions** – Never let them see you sweat – or cry, or explode in anger, or make any huge, uncontrolled display of emotion. It's just not professional. You don't have to be a robot, but keep your emotions in check and avoid letting your feelings get the best of you around your boss.

- **Take Constructive Criticism Well** – Your boss is there to manage you, which means helping you develop professionally and grow as an employee. Part of this job requires criticism of your work. Don't be defensive; keep an open mind. Then work to achieve even higher levels of competence and success.

The above strategies are great for working with most bosses; however, a few bosses require more finesse to manage. If you find yourself dealing with a boss who is a little more difficult than most, you're not alone. In fact, there are a few types of stereotypical bosses that nearly everyone will come in contact with over the course of his or her career. The following pages describe these, as well as important strategies to employ when dealing with each type.

The "Micro-Manager" Boss

A micro-manager boss is one who likes to control every detail of the work performed under his management. This kind of boss maintains tight control over information and resources, requires constant feedback on progress, seldom gives decision-making power or authority to others, can be closed to ideas, input or suggestions from subordinates, and tends to question employees about their decisions, methods and results.

Micro-manager bosses can be good to learn from early in your career because they usually provide detailed instructions and expectations, but often they are a source of frustration. They bottle-neck progress because every detail of your work requires their approval, they cause you to question your own abilities due to their lack of confidence in you, and they can make work tedious and more time-consuming than necessary.

If you find yourself dealing with a "Micro-Manager," try the following recommendations:

- Always restate your boss's expectations and concerns out loud so that she understands you hear her and comprehend your task.

- Ask specific questions, even if you think you know the answers, to prove you have the information needed to complete the job.

- Take notes in front of your boss. This demonstrates that you understand what your boss is saying is important.

- Try to anticipate your boss's questions and concerns and address them immediately. This will foster your boss's confidence in your ability to do the job and put her mind at ease.

- Provide regular feedback to your boss on your progress.

- Make sure to keep impeccable records of all of your work so that, if necessary, you are able to provide documentation of your work and justification for your decisions.

- Critique your own work. Is it possible that your boss is a micro-manager because she has little confidence in your work? Are you doing anything to encourage this lack of confidence?

The "Hands-Off" Boss

The hands-off boss wants his employees to think and act independently – often expecting little or no interaction with employees until a project is complete.

Because you are often left on your own, hands-off bosses can help you develop your own abilities quickly and can grant you great freedom in your work. On the other hand, hands-off bosses can also leave you feeling abandoned or frustrated due to lack of direction, feedback and constructive criticism.

To deal with the "Hands-Off" boss, try to:

- Gather as much information as possible from your boss at the start of a project. Ask lots of questions, confirm expectations, deadlines and consequences, and make sure you understand everything completely.

- Find other resources that can help you complete your work – co-workers, documents, books, Web sites, etc.

- Try to keep your contact with your boss to a minimum – don't seek feedback, ask unnecessary questions, or look for confirmation on your work until it is complete.

- Keep a meticulous record of your progress so that you can provide your boss with everything she needs to evaluate your work upon its completion.

The "Absentee" Boss

The absentee boss is the extreme version of the hands-off boss – and the exact opposite of the micro-manager boss. This kind of boss makes herself scarce – and can be hard to find when you need her. She expects business to carry on with or without her presence or help and needs employees to act independently.

Working for an absentee boss can give you a lot of freedom and can help you develop your confidence, decision making and independent thinking early in your career. On the other hand, an absentee boss offers little or no leadership, guidance or feedback, and often shuns his own responsibility – passing on the consequences of failures and mistakes directly to you.

To deal with an "Absentee" boss:

- Make communication with your boss top priority. If you know that she is only available for the first 20 minutes of the day, make sure you are there to speak with her.

- Monitor your own behavior. Without a boss breathing down your neck, it can be easy to take longer lunch breaks, defer work until tomorrow, or contribute work that is less than your best. You may get away with it, but it will only hurt you in the long run.

- Develop relationships with co-workers and other managers that you can rely on for guidance, advice and feedback.

The "I Want to be Your Friend" Boss

This kind of boss likes to avoid controversy and confrontation and will often go to great lengths to make sure her employees like her.

Working with this kind of boss can be a friendly and pleasant experience, and you can often develop a great relationship with this kind of boss that will serve you well in the future. However, you may find it difficult to get a clear picture of how well you are fulfilling your boss's expectations and you may also find it difficult to get her to address problems or deal with conflict that impedes your work.

To deal with the "I Want to be Your Friend" boss:

- Get a clear understanding of your boss's expectations at the outset of a project.

- Request regular feedback and advice from your boss as your work progresses.

- Use non-threatening methods to request professional criticism, such as telling your boss that you value her opinion and would like her honest evaluation, or by asking her to suggest ways you could improve.

- Praise your boss in front of co-workers, clients and other superiors. This kind of boss is concerned with your opinion of her and this kind of public accolade provides assurance that you respect and like her.

The "Under Qualified" Boss

This kind of boss worries that he lacks the experience, qualifications and credentials to be your boss – and he may be right. To fill in gaps in her capabilities, she may hire and rely on highly qualified employees and may believe her employees are so qualified that they need little or no guidance or feedback.

Working for an under qualified boss may give you opportunities to work on great projects and develop experience and skills that you otherwise might not have been able to develop until much later in your career. But working with a boss who is – or believes herself to be – under qualified may also cause you to miss out on learning from an experienced, confident and knowledgeable leader, and your work might suffer from lack of direction or input.

To deal with the "Under Qualified" boss:

- Develop a network of co-workers who can provide you help and feedback in the absence of your boss's ability to do so.

- Build your boss's trust and confidence by recognizing her accomplishments, abilities and experience in front of others.

- Use your boss's lack of confidence to your advantage by offering to help her with projects and tasks that you might otherwise not have gotten a chance to contribute to. This will help you develop your skills and experience, and will give your boss even greater trust in your abilities.

The "Over Achiever" Boss

The over achiever boss is a hard worker, perhaps even a workaholic – and expects her employees to work as hard, or harder, than she does. She expects the best and sets the bar high, always providing employees with what they need to succeed and expecting them to do so.

Working with an over achiever boss can be a great experience – they are usually qualified, competent leaders who challenge their employees to be the best they can be. However, they can also push employees too hard and expect too much – and come down hard on those who don't meet expectations.

To deal with the "Over Achiever" boss:

- Make sure you understand what is expected of you at the beginning of a project, and address any expectations that you feel might be unrealistic immediately.

- Request regular feedback and constructive criticism from your boss so that you can adequately gauge how your work is progressing.

- Take advantage of every opportunity you are given to improve yourself, and let your boss know you are interested in training seminars, extra projects, or other learning and growth experiences.

- Make sure your boss knows when you put in the extra effort or go the extra mile, like working late or over the weekend.

The "Threatened" Boss

This kind of boss is insecure and may even fear losing her job. To maximize her feelings of security, she tends to stick with the tried and true and discourages innovation or any form of "rocking the boat" from her employees. She rewards employees who follow directions, and reprimands those who do anything that is not status quo – especially if it is successful and outshines her own efforts.

There is little to be learned from a threatened boss; in fact, working for one can impede your career because you are given little opportunity to stand out or exhibit you own special talents and skills.

To deal with the "Threatened" boss:

- Build your boss's trust by recognizing her accomplishments and experience in front of others.

- Complete your projects as your boss has requested.

- Keep a careful record of your work in case your boss tries to take credit for your work or undermine you.

- Build relationships with other managers so you do not end up isolated by your boss.

Handling and Resolving Conflicts

Conflicts are unavoidable in life – and work is no different. You can expect that, from time to time, you and your boss will not see eye to eye. Occasional conflicts with your boss aren't the end of the world; in fact, learning how to handle these conflicts is an important learning experience and can actually lead to a closer and more productive relationship with your boss. To constructively deal with conflict between you and your boss:

- **Pick Your Battles** – Make sure what you are upset about is really worth pursuing. Are you upset that your boss forgot your birthday during a stressful week at work? Probably not worth making a stink over. Did she accidentally take credit for one of your accomplishments in front of an important client? This may be something you need to discuss.

- **Address Problems as They Occur** – Don't sit and stew. If something is bothering you, or you suspect that something is bothering your boss, address it right away.

- **Have an Honest Discussion** – Ask your boss to sit down for a meeting. Find out what's expected of you and how you can meet those expectations – especially in relation to the specific conflict you are having. Getting feedback may be all you need.

- **Keep Records** – Keep a meticulous record of all of your work – e-mails, phone calls, client interactions, documents, reports, etc. If your boss has a problem with your work or accuses you of something that is not true, you will have the evidence to back up your claims.

- **Control Yourself** – Yelling, crying or generally making a scene is never a good policy. It's unprofessional and makes you look like a loose cannon.

- **Look for Support** – If you are having a specific problem with your boss or just have problems with her in general, look to a co-worker or mentor for guidance. An unbiased, outside opinion may help you put the problem in perspective or give you the input you need to develop a strategy to deal with it. Others at your company might also know added history or motivation for your boss's behavior. Just make sure you conduct yourself professionally and never reduce yourself to gossiping about the boss or criticizing her to someone who may leak the information.

- **Know Your Rights** – The boss isn't always right. Employees have rights and you don't have to put up with behavior that violates your rights, is over the top, or is generally offensive. If you know your rights, you will know when they've been violated – and what recourse you have.

- **Go to the Top** – Sometimes a relationship with a boss really stinks. If the problem is extreme, you may have to talk to your boss's boss, or a representative from human resources. Just make sure that the problem truly warrants this extreme action.

Sometimes you just have to face that you can't control your boss. But don't let an uncomfortable situation at work make your entire life miserable. If you truly can't get along with your boss, try focusing on what you can control:

- Focus on what you like about your job. Perhaps the work is exciting, the pay is good, and/or you like your co-workers. Your boss isn't the only part of your job that makes it worthwhile.

- Don't give your boss anything to complain about. Be on time. Don't complain. Complete work by deadline. Be a team player. Meet or exceed expectations. If you don't give your boss anything to create a conflict about, you'll have less conflict overall.

- Gain perspective. Realize what is important in your life; your job and what your boss thinks of you don't define you completely. Develop interests and activities outside of work that help you create the life you want.

- Admit when it's time for a change. If you've tried many approaches and nothing you do has improved the situation, it may be time to consider looking for employment elsewhere. A mismatch between you and your boss in personalities, values, management style and corporate culture are all legitimate concerns that might warrant a change in employment.

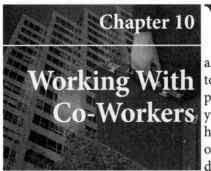

Chapter 10

Working With Co-Workers

Your co-workers can have a significant impact on your job satisfaction, job performance, and long-term career goals. In order to succeed at work, you need to create positive, productive relationships with your colleagues. You also need to learn how to deal with all kinds of related obstacles and situations, from how to deal with difficult personalities to what to do if you fall in love with a co-worker. The following pages describe what you can do to get – and keep – your relationships with the people with whom you work on track.

Creating Positive Relationships with Co-workers

As the new kid on the block, your co-workers will wonder what to make of you. Can they trust you? Will you contribute to the team? Will you make their job easier or more difficult? Are you positive and fun? Can they depend on you to do your job, make good decisions, and be trustworthy?

It will take some time for you to get to know your co-workers and to prove yourself to them. But, there are some things you can begin to do right off the bat to earn your co-workers' respect, support and goodwill.

- **Do Your Job** – Understand the expectations of your job and meet them. Be responsible, dependable and trustworthy. Do your best in every aspect of your job and contribute your fair share and then some. If you do your job well, it will make your co-workers' jobs easier and they will come to understand that they can count on you.

- **Be Considerate and Thoughtful** – Keep in mind how your behavior affects others. Live by the golden rule – treat others as you would like to be treated. Share. Clean up after yourself. Help your co-workers when you can –even if it's not in your job description. Remember people's birthdays and ask your co-workers how they are doing. A little consideration and thoughtfulness goes a long way.

- **Value Your Co-workers** – Let your co-workers know that you value their contributions, intelligence and experience and compliment them whenever appropriate – and in front of others. Ask them for advice to show them that you respect their opinion. You can learn a lot from their experience and perspective.

- **Be Positive** – Nobody likes a complainer. If you don't have anything good to say, don't say anything at all. And, if you must criticize, be constructive and diplomatic.

- **Be Modest** – Nobody likes a braggart. Learn how to effectively showcase your strengths and achievements without bragging or putting others down.

- **Respect Others** – Your co-workers will come from all walks of life and will have diverse opinions, experience and perspectives. Understand that not everyone will have the same ideas as you and respect their differences.

- **Play Fair** – It's a stark fact of work life: most of the time, in one way or another, you are in competition with your co-workers. For that promotion, for the boss's attention, for performance-based bonuses and incentives, you will probably have many opportunities to personally benefit by playing dirty – but don't give in to the temptation. Discrediting others for personal gain isn't fair, it isn't nice, and it isn't going to earn you any respect.

- **Be Social** – It's a good idea to keep your work life and personal life separate, but that doesn't mean you have to be anti-social. Have lunch with co-workers, engage in water cooler conversations, show interest in others, and reveal some things about yourself so that your co-workers feel that they know you.

- **Avoid Conflict** – Conflict is a natural – and unavoidable – part of work. In fact, conflict is often how ideas are generated, problems are solved and innovations are forged. However, you should avoid non-productive conflicts. If you sense a conflict arising, address the situation immediately and take appropriate actions to resolve it.

Office Friendships

Friendships are common at work – just look at all the popular television shows that focus on the relationships of people who work together. Research shows that people who consider their co-workers friends experience more job satisfaction and higher productivity. And, after several years on the job, many people count their relationships with co-workers as their closest and most satisfying. But there's a flip side to office friendships as well.

At their best, office friendships promote goodwill among employees, improve communication, foster healthy competition and generally make the office a better and more fun place to work. At their worst, office friendships can wreak havoc on an office environment – and on your career – by breeding backstabbing, gossip, hurt feelings, bad attitudes, aggressive competition, and sabotage.

Unlike friendships you form with schoolmates, neighbors and other acquaintances, work friendships come with the caveat that something is always at stake – your career. You can – and should – develop healthy and fulfilling friendships with co-workers – just keep a few things in mind:

- **Remember What's at Stake** – If your pal at the gym or your old college roommate decides not to be your friend anymore, you may be sad, but when a work friendship goes bad, it can make your work life uncomfortable – or downright excruciating. Your former friend could tell other co-workers – or even a boss – unflattering things about you. You might even find yourself in competition for a prime assignment or promotion with your former friend , who will likely be less willing to play fair since your friendship went south. You don't just have a friendship at stake – you have your career on the line as well.

- **Proceed with Caution** – You make think that your best friend at work is truly a best friend, and he or she might be. But research shows that it takes about three years for people to make fair judgments about whether someone is a true friend or not. So ask yourself: do you really know your co-worker as well as you think you do? Don't make the mistake of trusting someone with your career before you actually know them.

- **Establish Boundaries** – Don't forget that your work friends work where you do and can have an influence on your career. It's best to establish boundaries for your office friendships that include what personal details you will reveal (does your office mate really need to know that you were almost arrested for streaking with your fraternity during college?), what subjects you will talk about (talking about last night's episode of Law and Order – good. Talking about other people you work with – bad.), and what kinds of activities you will engage in together. The last thing you need is to reveal something embarrassing about yourself or say something mean about a co-worker, then have it spread around the office after a friendship sours.

- **Be Thoughtful** – It's great to have friends, but try to be mindful that not everybody makes friends easily. It's easy to create a circle of work friends that becomes a clique, which makes other co-workers feel left out. Avoid hurt feelings by including others as much as possible, by keeping "inside jokes" and information to a minimum, and by refusing to engage in hurtful gossip. Office cliques are a subtle form of bullying, and you don't want to be seen by co-workers and managers as a bully.

- **Think Long Term** – You and your work friend might work in the same department and capacity now, but that might not always be so. Remember that you may one day be promoted and actually be your friend's manager, or vice versa. Conduct all of your work friendships in a way that will make transitions as comfortable as possible.

- **Remember That Appearances Do Count** – It may not be fair, but people do make judgments about you based on appearances. If you are always going to lunch with the same co-worker of the opposite sex, others might deduce that you are dating – even if your co-worker is married. And if you strike up a close friendship with a superior, others might assume that your promotion was a result of your relationship. You don't have to be paranoid, but just keep in mind that people do talk – and try not to give them anything to talk about when it comes to you.

- **Diversify** – Don't invest your entire emotional and social life in your work. Make sure that the friends you have at the office are just one part of your circle. That way, if office friendships expire, it won't be devastating. Plus, it will help you establish and maintain healthy boundaries with your office friends if you don't rely on them for everything.

Office Romances

Romance at the office is commonplace these days. How can it not be? In many cases, people spend more time at work interacting with co-workers than they do at home with family and friends. We'd be kidding ourselves if we thought that we could spend that much time with each other and not have a few romances bloom. But, just because office romance is common it's not always accepted. Even if it is accepted at your company, there are still some ground rules you should follow. To keep your career – and your heart – in one piece:

- **Follow the Rules** – Many companies have policies that outline what is and is not allowed when it comes to relationships between co-workers. Or, your company may allow it, but require you to disclose it to a manager. Your company may forbid any romantic relationships between co-workers. Even if your company does allow romantic relationships, remember that there are other rules to follow as well (married or otherwise committed co-workers are off limits, for instance).

- **Keep it Professional** – Sure, you may be drunk with love, but nobody at work wants to hear you call your significant other "hunny bear" or watch public displays of affection. Keep in mind how your relationship may affect others at the office, and maintain professionalism at all times.

- **Keep it on Even Ground** – Romantic relationships between managers and those they manage is strictly off limits, and usually prohibited by most companies. When the power balance is off in a relationship there's too much at stake, including careers and reputations. As the manager, you don't want to be accused of playing favorites with the one you love, or be accused of sexual harassment if the relationship sours. As the subordinate, you don't want your achievements to be seen as a result of your romantic relationship with the boss – it will destroy your credibility and breed contempt with co-workers.

- **Be Discreet but not Secretive** – It's nearly impossible to keep a secret at the office, so don't even try – you'll appear to be dishonest or ashamed of your behavior and might incur more gossip. That said, you also don't have to scream your love from the mountaintop. It's probably best to disclose your relationship to management and to be honest should co-workers ask about it, but don't make your relationship the topic of every conversation.

- **Keep in Touch with Reality** – The truth of the matter is that most dating relationships end in a break up. You might think that this relationship is "the one," but it may not be. Try to conduct your relationship in a way that won't embarrass you or make you feel uncomfortable should it end. Remember: even if the relationship ends, your employment doesn't and you may have to work with your ex for years to come.

Difficult Co-Workers

Throughout life, you will encounter people who are difficult to deal with, and the work place is no different. Even though we hope that our co-workers will be friendly, helpful and fun, that's not always the case. From the simply annoying to the downright nasty, you will come across your share of difficult coworkers in the course of your career. You don't have to let these no-good co-workers bring you down. By recognizing some common personality types and learning how to deal with them, you can head off trouble and keep your career on track.

- **Chatty Cathy – or Charles** – This co-worker is well meaning, but annoying, and is often a productivity killer. He views his constant conversation as proof that he is a team player, but if the babble doesn't drive you crazy, the extra hours you'll spend making up for time lost while listening will.

What to do: *Try creating barriers that give the message that you're not available to chat – a closed door, for example – and try to head off talks by looking busy when you see this person coming your way (pick up the phone, or start typing like crazy). Don't encourage conversation – keep your answers to one word. And, if all else fails, have an honest but kind discussion – something along the lines of, "I really do like talking to you, but I find that I fall behind on my work when we talk too much. Let's try keeping our talks to a few minutes in the morning before work starts, or during our lunch break."*

- **The Slacker** – At one time or another, you will have someone in your department or on your team who is unable – or unwilling – to contribute in any meaningful way. This person might not have sufficient skills or education, may be disorganized or a procrastinator, could be insecure, or might just be lazy and willing to let someone else take up the slack. Whatever the reason, this co-worker will likely make you work harder to make up for his or her shortcomings – and will make you mad in the process. This person might even take credit for your work when it's all said and done!

  What to do: *Keep your nose to the grindstone. If you do your work and do it well, those in charge will realize where the fault lies. That said, don't try to make excuses for the slacker, and do everything you can to make her accountable for her actions and shortcomings. If the boss asks why a project missed deadline or didn't meet expectations, be honest but diplomatic.*

- **The Gossiper** – This co-worker is trouble – and will stop at nothing to make himself look better by discrediting others. He may seem friendly and fun at first, but only because he's trying to engage you in a conversation that he will mine for tidbits to use against you. Nothing is off limits with this guy – from attacking your work ethic, to disclosing your personal information, to outright lying.

  What to do: *Take the high road by refusing to engage in the gossip's game. Don't give the gossip anything to talk about; act professionally and prove his attacks wrong with your skills, dedication and performance. If you're a stellar employee, the gossip won't have anything to say – and won't be believed even if he does.*

- **Mr. Toxic** – A chronic complainer, if Mr. Toxic is going to say anything, it's going to be negative. This is the co-worker who immediately brings the mood of a room down.

  What to do: *Don't let this person get to you, and don't let him get too far. When he opens his mouth, do what you can to cut him short, and try to counteract his negativity by being enthusiastic, complimentary and positive.*

- **The Brown Noser** – Everyone knows what a brown noser is, and everyone detests this type. Unfortunately, most offices have one. From spying on co-workers and reporting to the boss, to buying expensive holiday and birthday gifts for managers, this person will stop at nothing to gain a superior's attention and favor.

  What to do: *Don't give the brown noser any ammunition to take to the boss, but, mostly, ignore her. Most people can see a brown noser coming for miles, and if you perform well, it will be noticed – despite the brown noser's attempts to outdo you.*

In general, when dealing with difficult co-workers, you should keep the following tips in mind:

- Accept that you and your co-workers are different and that you will have differences of opinion.

- Keep calm. Overt anger or frustration will only escalate the situation.

- Figure out what the source of the conflict is. Why do you find this person difficult? What bothers you about him/her?

- Keep it in perspective. Is your office mate's annoying habit of eating your food really worth possibly compromising your career?

- Create some solutions that you think will work.

- Discuss the situation with your co-worker. In many cases, just talking about the problem may resolve it. Perhaps your co-worker doesn't know he's being difficult – or maybe there are factors in play that you are unaware of that help explain his behavior.

- If you have tried but are unable to resolve problems with co-workers on your own, don't let it get out of control. Take your conflict to your manager or to human resources for some mediation.

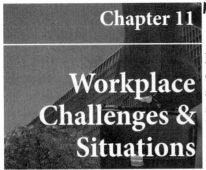

Chapter 11

Workplace Challenges & Situations

The path to success includes challenges, problems and missteps – and you need to know how to handle them if you are going to stay on track. Resilience, flexibility and the ability to deal effectively with adversity are the hallmarks of a successful person. Unfortunately, these things are not taught in school – they must be learned through experience. There are, however, some tips that can help you tackle the challenges you face in your career with grace. Here are a few.

Making Mistakes

Mistakes happen. While nobody wants to make mistakes, successful people learn from their missteps. If handled badly, mistakes can have a negative impact on your career. If handled well, you can learn from your mistakes, gain valuable experience and really prove yourself as someone who can overcome adversity. Here's how:

- **Be Accountable** – Own up to your mistakes immediately. Don't hope that no one will notice or that it will somehow go away if you ignore it. The longer you wait to accept responsibility, the worse the situation is likely to get.

- **Apologize, but Don't Make Excuses** – A sincere apology is necessary, but a litany of why the mistake was made or why it wasn't your fault is not.

- **Learn from the Mistake** – Evaluate what you did wrong, how you handled the situation, and what you can do different next time to avoid the same snafu.

- **Avoid Careless Mistakes** – You are going to make mistakes no matter how hard you try not to, but that doesn't mean you should just throw your hands up and be careless. Most mistakes are avoidable, so take control when possible.

- **Don't Beat Yourself Up** – You've made a mistake, you've dealt with it the best you can – now forgive yourself and move on. There's nothing to be gained by dwelling on your mistake or becoming angry.

Embarrassment

Embarrassment is awkward, uncomfortable and unpleasant – but part of life. If you do or say something embarrassing (or someone else does), you can't go back in time and change it, but there are things you can do to minimize the negative impact of the moment.

- **Maintain Your Composure** – By maintaining control and acting confident and respectful, you will show others that you are not easily shaken.

- **Avoid Drawing Attention to Other People's Embarrassment** – If someone else embarrasses him or herself, do what you can to divert attention from the situation and minimize the embarrassment. However, if the person tries to use humor to diffuse the situation, laugh with him.

- **Don't Apologize or Make Excuses** – Everyone knows what it feels like to be embarrassed, so an apology is probably not necessary – and may even make others feel even more uncomfortable. Just regain your composure and move on.

Boredom

At times, you may find that you are bored at work. Being bored from time to time isn't a big problem, but if you have lost your overall enthusiasm and passion for your job and find yourself settled into a mundane and uninteresting routine, your boredom can escalate into frequent absences, poor performance and dissatisfaction with your career. Try the following to alleviate your boredom:

- **Break up Mundane Tasks with Exciting Ones** – If you spend days on end filing, you are bound to get bored. Instead, file for a few minutes every day and spend the rest of your day on the more interesting and creative aspects of your job.

- **Volunteer for New Projects** – Even if it is something as small as volunteering to plan the office holiday party, or joining a committee, adding new responsibilities and challenges to your daily routine can go a long way toward spicing up your work day. Plus, you might find that you have talents you were unaware of or interests in different kinds of work.

- **Discuss Your Situation with Your Boss** – Don't tell your boss that you're "bored." Instead, let him know that you are available to take on new challenges and interested in trying new things.

- **Consider a Change** – Of course, if you've tried everything and still find that you are bored with your job, you may need to seek employment that is more challenging and better suited to your skills and talents. Just make sure it's actually your job and not your attitude or something else – otherwise you might find a new job is similarly unfulfilling.

Motivation

In the early days of your career, you will be so excited by the novelty of your new job and so overwhelmed by everything you have to learn, it may be hard to believe that you will ever have a problem keeping yourself motivated. But, it happens to the best of us – even if we love our job and are generally happy with our career. Whether you experience a temporary rut or find that you are having more long-term problems with staying passionate and motivated in your career, there are some things you can do to boost your attitude.

- **Add Fun and Variety to Your Work Routine** – Whether it's adding a joke of the day calendar to your desk or volunteering to complete a task that is outside of your normal responsibilities, small things can add an element of surprise and joy to your day.

- **Seek Leadership Roles at Your Company** – Leading projects and people will give you a sense of purpose.

- **Develop Ownership of Your Work** – Take responsibility for your mistakes – and for your accomplishments. Know that you really do control the outcome of your career.

- **Concentrate on Your Goals and the Big Picture** – Remind yourself how your work – no matter how mundane or boring – is contributing to the mission of your company and helping you to develop valuable skills and experience.

- **Seek Feedback from Supervisors and Colleagues** – Positive feedback will make you feel good, and constructive criticism will help you set goals.

- **Maintain a Positive Attitude** – The way you look at things really does affect the way you feel. When you finish a task, tell yourself you did a great job. Smile and give people compliments. Don't be too hard on yourself – or others.

- **Find Something at Work to be Grateful for Each Day** – Did your office mate tell a great story? Was the coffee particularly good today? Did you get a compliment from your boss on the success of a recent project?

Handling Criticism

Receiving criticism is part of any career. It's not fun, but it's necessary. Whether the criticism is negative or positive, coming from a supervisor or from co-workers, directed at your work skills or personal skills, it can help you understand your shortcomings and encourage you to improve. When you receive criticism, do the following:

- **Listen** – As you are receiving criticism, don't interrupt. Let the person finish to make sure you are getting all of the information.

- **Stay Calm** – Getting angry or defensive will only irritate the other person and make you appear uncooperative and unwilling to take criticism.

- **Make Sure You Understand** – Confirm what you have heard to make sure you got all of the points.

- **Seek Privacy** – Being criticized in public is not acceptable. If you find yourself in this situation, calmly ask the person if you can continue the situation somewhere private. If the person refuses, you may have to consider cutting the conversation short and continuing later in private.

Stress

Stress is a normal part of life. In fact, stress can be positive – it motivates us, keeps us on our toes, and drives us to find new and better ways of doing things. It's only when a person doesn't know how to deal well with stress that it becomes unhealthy. The symptoms of stress include:

- **Physical** – Weight loss or gain, headaches, fatigue, changes in sleep patterns, stomach problems, muscle aches and tightness.

- **Emotional** – Easily angered or frustrated, nervousness, irritability, mood swings.

- **Mental** – Confusion, lack of interest in favorite activities, loss of concentration, forgetfulness.

You will have your fair share of stress in your job. How you manage this stress will determine your success. Here's how:

- **Identify Your Stressors** – Determine what stresses you out so you can deal with it. Hate being late? Make sure you plan more than enough time to do everything. Freak out when you have to give reports at meetings? Take a public speaking class.

- **Manage Your Time** – A lot of stress results from not having enough time to complete tasks. Keep a calendar and a running to-do list to help you manage your time, and make sure that you fairly assess how much time it will take you to complete something – then add 15 minutes to make up for unplanned interruptions.

- **Organize** – A lot of stress also results from disorganization. When you can't find things, don't have set systems for dealing with situations, and are generally disorganized, you add a lot of unnecessary stress to your life.

- **Prioritize** – If you make everything a top priority you'll go crazy. Decide what is really important and what can slide.

- **Ask for Help and Learn how to say No** – Asking for help isn't a sign of weakness – it's a sign of leadership. Learn to delegate and don't take on more than you can handle.

- **Avoid Procrastination** – It's easy to put off things that you don't find enjoyable, but often you will find that the task becomes even more unsavory when you are late, have less time to complete it, and are under pressure. Set deadlines and stick to them.

- **Take Time for Yourself** – You need to take time to take care of yourself. Take breaks throughout the day, take vacations, and fill your nights and weekends with things you enjoy, like hobbies and friends.

- **Keep Your Perspective** – It may feel like the world will end if you don't finish that report on time – but it's unlikely. When you are feeling really stressed, take a step back and ask yourself how the situation will really affect you or others. Will you lose your job? Will someone die? Will it affect your life for years to come? Probably not. In fact, in two months you will most likely have forgotten all about it. Putting things in perspective is an instant stress reliever.

- **Create a Strong Support Network** – Having friends, mentors and supporter is important to handling stress. When you have someone to vent to, ask advice from, and laugh with, you don't feel alone in your stress.

- **Get Professional Guidance** – If you feel that your stress is out of control, you may need professional help in learning to deal with it. Seeing a counselor is one option, but you may also consider taking a class in meditation or taking a seminar in stress reduction.

Burnout

Burnout is serious emotional exhaustion resulting from your job. It's not uncommon – most people experience it at some time during their career – but it can be serious. People who have job burnout lose interest in their jobs, stop giving their best effort to their work, often experience emotional and physical turmoil that affects their quality of life, and may even end up losing their job. If you suspect you may be experiencing job burnout, ask yourself the following questions:

- Do you dread going to work?

- Do you find yourself longing for Friday night all week long and feel a sense of dread on Sunday afternoons because you know you must return to work the next day?

- Do you do the bare minimum at work and just coast along, but still feel drained at the end of the day?

- Are you experiencing health problems like headaches, stomachaches and fatigue?

- Do you feel irritable, moody and resentful when it comes to work?

- Do you find that you no longer enjoy parts of your job that used to be a pleasure?

- Are you jealous and resentful toward people who claim to love their job?

- Do you lose your temper easily?

If you can answer yes to one or more of these questions, you may be on the track to job burnout.

People who work under a lot of job stress, are fearful of losing their job, work with a "toxic" supervisor or coworkers, or are working at a company undergoing a lot of change or turmoil (layoffs, bankruptcy or scandal, for example) are prime candidates for job burnout. But burnout can happen to anyone. Here's how to deal with it:

- **Admit It** – If you are feeling burned out, admit it so you can take the steps to fix it. Pretending that everything is okay will just make things worse.

- **Take Care of Yourself** – Eat right, get enough sleep, exercise and see a doctor regularly. Feeling bad can contribute to job burnout or make it worse.

- **Nurture Your Relationships at Work and Beyond** – Having a strong support system of coworkers, friends and family can help you cope with the stresses of your job.

- **Take a Break** – Make sure you use your vacation time, take sick days when you aren't well, and take regular breaks throughout the day to do something you enjoy – eat at the great deli on the corner, sit in the sun for a few minutes, or read a chapter of a book.

- **Draw the Line** – Burnout often occurs when a person doesn't know how to stop working. Make a commitment that you will not take work home with you on a regular basis, that you won't check your e-mail at midnight, that you will turn your cell phone off after a certain time, and that you will begin to set limits on how much you are willing to give and do at work. Work can't be your entire life.

- **Make Time for Fun** – Whether it's planning a fun Friday lunch for coworkers, forwarding a great joke to your office mates, or taking up rock climbing on the weekends, taking time to laugh and have fun can really recharge your batteries.

- **Communicate** – Let your supervisors and co-workers know, in a positive way, that you are making changes to help you refocus on your work. Find someone you can vent to and use as a sounding board.

- **Prioritize** – People get burned out when they are perfectionists and try to do everything. Be realistic about what you can accomplish, and make real decisions about what is really important to you and what things you can let slide – both at work and at home.

- **Reclaim Your Power by Making a Plan** – You are not powerless over your work or your life. Set goals and make a plan for how you will create the kind of work life you want. Maybe this includes more education, a new position, a new attitude, or even a new job.

- **Face that it Might be Time to Move on** – Burnout doesn't necessarily mean that you are in the wrong career, the wrong position, or at the wrong company – but it can. If you have come to realize that you have chosen a career that is all wrong for you, that your position doesn't fit you or your skills at all, or that your company has a culture that doesn't fit with your values, don't try to fit a round peg into a square hole. Make a plan for moving on – and then do it.

Chapter 12

Teamwork

Traditionally, decisions in the workplace were made by managers and employees were rewarded and recognized for individual achievement. Today's work culture, however, understands that working together as teams encourages creativity, productivity and responsibility, and companies recognize and reward employees who are team players.

Being a team player comes easy for some people; for others it may be more difficult. Shyness, lack of confidence, an inability to surrender control or delegate, or an unwillingness to give up individual recognition to work for the greater good – all of these traits can impede successful teams.

But even if working on a team doesn't come naturally for you, you can develop your inner team player. Here's how:

What a Team is

A team is a collection of two or more people working interdependently toward a common goal and a shared reward. The part that should be emphasized, however, is working together. Anybody can throw a group of people together and tell them they have to get something done; a genuine team, however, works collaboratively to achieve better results than they would have attained individually. Members of successful teams are:

- Galvanized by a common goal
- Able to overcome their need for individual recognition in order to work for the team's success
- Able to value diversity and capitalize on the strengths of fellow team members
- Focused on action rather than duty or a fear of failure

Teams that fail fall victim to inaction, poor communication, lack of leadership or sense of common mission. In addition, egos, conflicting goals and competition between members for recognition and rewards can destroy a team.

A true team, then, can be defined as a group of people who work together successfully and who have a common, well-understood purpose, specific goals, and a feeling of personal investment in the team's success – even above their own personal interest.

How a Successful Team Works

You understand that today's corporate culture has invested in the idea that teams can achieve greater success than individuals. You know that you will be expected to work on a team, and hopefully you are even excited about the idea. But how exactly do teams work? It's something you need to understand in order to contribute fully to a strong team.

Successful teams at work are not unlike successful sports teams; in fact, they share many of the same characteristics. Think about what you know about championship teams. What do these teams have in common? What is important to their success? Chances are, the same traits that make your favorite sports team successful also help build successful teams at work. These traits include:

- **Clear Expectations and Consequences** – To succeed, teams must fully understand what is expected of them, what outcomes they must produce, and the consequences of not achieving those goals.

- **Defined Purpose** – Team members should understand why a team has been formed and why they have been chosen to participate. They must also realize how the work of the team fits into the big picture of the company's overall vision.

- **Strategy** – Teams must have leadership, a framework for how work will be completed, a clear decision-making and conflict resolution process, defined roles, and a system by which progress and success will be measured. In other words, teams must develop a strategy by which they will reach goals, complete work and achieve success.

- **Communication, Collaboration and Compromise** – Quite simply, a team that works well knows how to communicate, work together, and compromise for the greater good.

- **Creativity and Innovation** – Teams understand that creative thinking, unique solutions, and new ideas are the foundation for success and they reward members for creativity and innovation. On a team, members understand that they can take reasonable risks and challenge the status quo.

- **Empowerment** – In order to truly succeed, teams must feel that their work will be valued, that their success will have an impact on the company, and that they have the resources and authority necessary to achieve success.

- **Accountability** – It's never one person's fault if a team fails – every team member has a responsibility in the results.

- **Overall Culture that Values Teams** – Teams that work well are part of companies that recognize the benefits of a team culture is over that of a traditional, hierarchical organization. Companies that believe in team culture provide the resources, authority, and rewards necessary to build successful teams.

How to be a Team Player

Understanding the profile of a team player is the first step to being one. Every team is different, and every individual contributes in their own way, but generally a team player is:

- **Reliable** – Team players can be counted on to meet deadlines, complete work that meets expectations and follow through on commitments. Team players earn and maintain the trust of their teammates.

- **A Good Communicator** – Team players are able to communicate ideas and opinions effectively. They are also good at listening – which is equally, if not more, important to good communication.

- **Eager to Participate at all Levels** - A team player is an enthusiastic and willing participant in the work of the team and doesn't get hung up on whether work is "beneath them," outside of his/her job description, or someone else's responsibility. A true team player is willing to pitch in to do anything – from serving as a leader, to doing small administrative tasks.

- **Willing to Share Ideas, Experience and Resources** – A team player is invested in the success of the team and is willing to selflessly contribute – even if it means he or she might not receive individual recognition or reward.

- **Receptive and Respectful of Different Ideas and Perspectives** – A team player understands that diversity is a strength, and exhibits respect and appreciation for other experiences, ideas and points of view.

- **Cooperative and Willing to Compromise** – Teams are built on the idea that "none of us are as strong as all of us." Team players understand that to fully capitalize on the strength of a team, cooperation and compromise are necessary.

- **Flexible** – Not everything goes as planned. A team player understands that flexibility is necessary when it comes to accommodating the needs of others, and in overcoming unanticipated circumstances and problems.

- **A Believer in Personal Responsibility** – Team players aren't finger pointers – they understand that being a member of a team means owning up to mistakes, taking fair share of the blame when failure occurs – and enjoying fair share of the rewards when the team succeeds.

- **A Problem Solver** – A team player doesn't complain or worry about whose fault it is – he just solves the problem and gets the work done.

- **Respectful and Supportive of Team Members** – A team player genuinely cares about team members and gives them the respect, empathy, and support they need.

- **Committed to the Success of the Team** – Team players value the success of the team above all else – even personal gain – and are willing to put in the work to achieve this success.

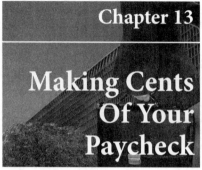

Chapter 13

Making Cents Of Your Paycheck

I t's one of the greatest rewards of working – your paycheck. From the moment you started college, you probably began fantasizing about what you would do with all that money you will make when you finish – a luxury car, vacations, a mansion on the hill. It may be quite a shock, then, when you open your first paycheck to find it is substantially less than you had expected. Why? Deductions! From Federal income and Social Security taxes, to health insurance and flexible spending accounts, deductions from your paycheck can really add up. In the end, you may find that your paycheck is just 50-60 percent of what you actually earned.

Don't just ignore those deductions noted on your paycheck with strange abbreviations. Understanding where your money goes will not only make your smaller paycheck easier to swallow, but also protect you from potential accounting mistakes. In addition, by understanding where the funds from your paycheck are going, you can develop strategies to minimize deductions, from choosing the right number of allowances on your W-4 form to selecting the appropriate insurance plans for your needs.

Typical Deductions

As mentioned before, there are various types of deductions that can reduce the amount of "take-home" funds. Typical deductions from your paycheck include:

Federal Income Taxes

Federal income taxes take the heftiest chunk of cash from your paycheck. These funds go into a pot that pays for things that our elected leaders have deemed as necessary, such as military to protect our country, social programs like food stamps and Medicare, and divisions of the government like the Department of Education, the Department of Agriculture and the Department of Homeland Security.

The most confusing thing about Federal income taxes is the fact that different tax rates apply depending on your specific circumstances. This is because the Federal government uses a "progressive" tax system: taxable income levels are divided into brackets with lowest income brackets paying the least amount of tax. Tax brackets currently start at 10 percent and go to 35 percent. The more you earn, the more you pay.

So how does the progressive tax system work? Let's pretend for a moment that you were single and you had a total income of $51,550 in 2005. Not adjusting for deductions and credits, your taxes in 2005 would be calculated in the following manner:

Applicable Tax Brackets	Tax Owed
10 percent tax on the first $7,300	$ 730
15 percent tax on the next $22,399	$3,360
25 percent tax on the next $21,851	$5,463
Total Tax Owed	**$9,553**

Current tax rate schedules are available online at www.irs.gov

Of course, adjustments, deductions and credits can significantly impact the amount of taxes you pay. For example, if you have children, make mortgage payments, or make contributions to charities, your tax bill will be lower. You actually have the ability to give the Federal government recommendations on how much money to take out of your paycheck through the W-4 form, a form you fill out on the first day you arrive at your new job. This form allows you to indicate the number of "allowances" you claim. Allowances are those factors that may lead you, at the end of the year, to pay less in taxes (like owning a home, having children, etc.).

In most cases, as a new graduate, you would probably claim one allowance on your W-4 form. Claiming zero will cause you to pay more in taxes and will probably result in a refund at the end of the year. Claiming two or higher will cause less taxes to be taken out of your monthly paycheck, but might mean you will owe taxes at the end of the year.

Keep in mind that although receiving a big tax refund check from the government may seem like a good thing, it's not. That money was yours all along. Why let the government keep it all year long, when you could use it or put it in an investment account and earn interest on it? Therefore, it's in your best interest to monitor your taxes year to year to determine the correct amount that should be deducted from your paycheck so that you avoid the big tax refund or, worse, a big tax bill. A tax professional can assist you with this.

State and Local Taxes

The Federal government isn't the only agency that needs your money to operate. Most (although not all) states, and some municipalities, also require citizens to pay income taxes to support their operations. Some use a progressive tax rate, similar in concept to the Federal government's, while others use a flat tax system where everyone pays the same percentage of their income, regardless of how much money they earn. To find out more about your local situation, contact your state and local government offices or consult with a local accountant.

Social Security and Medicare Taxes

As a United States citizen, you are required pay social security and Medicare taxes on your wages – commonly referred to as FICA (Federal Insurance Contributions Act). These taxes are used to fund retirement income and health insurance to citizens 65 and over. Currently, every worker is required to contribute 12.4 percent of his/her annual income to social security and an additional 2.9 percent to Medicare. In most cases, you pay half of this tax and your employer is required to pay the other half. However, if you are self-employed, you are required to pay the entire amount (commonly referred to as the Self-Employment Tax).

Insurance Deductions

Many companies provide employees reduced cost insurance as a benefit of employment. This can include health, dental, vision, disability, and supplemental insurance. To receive this benefit, you agree to pay a portion of the insurance expense – commonly 50 percent. Therefore, if your insurance plan costs $4,680.00 per year and your employer agrees to pay half, the rest will be deducted from your paycheck. If you are paid on a weekly basis, it will be deducted over 52 weeks, so $45.00 will be deducted from each of your paychecks.

In some cases, your employer may offer you a variety of reduced cost insurance programs. These are described in more detail in the next chapter. If you are fortunate enough to receive reduced cost insurance options from your employer, you should seriously consider taking advantage of these options, as insurance can be very expensive. Of course, always be sure to weigh the benefits of each plan and select the program that fits your needs.

Other Deductions

There are a variety of other deductions that could affect your paycheck. Some companies charge for parking, which is then deducted from paychecks. Some companies offer flexible spending accounts for medical purposes or child care expenses, in which funds are deducted from your paycheck without being taxed by the government, then deposited into an account and reimbursed to you as you provide receipts of medical bills and/or child care costs. Because you don't pay taxes on this money, it saves you money. Your company may ask employees to donate to fundraising campaigns for organizations such as United Way or Red Cross, and, if you choose to participate, your donation is deducted from your paycheck.

Reviewing Your Paycheck

Always make a point to review every pay stub you receive to ensure that you understand all the deductions that are being applied to your paycheck. If you do not understand what a deduction is for, or how the amount of a specific deduction was determined, contact your payroll department. Remember, it's your money – you should know where it is going.

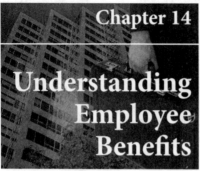

Chapter 14

Understanding Employee Benefits

When evaluating the value of your job, your salary is really only half of the picture. In fact, the other half of the picture – your benefits – can be just as important to your quality of life as the amount of money you make.

These days, most full-time employees receive some form of health insurance programs, retirement plans and paid leave. Some companies even offer free or reduced cost childcare, free gym memberships, paid leave for new parents, access to free or reduced cost education, and flexible work hours. However, in this age of rising insurance costs and shrinking profits, it is becoming more difficult for employers to offer all the benefits they would like. In fact, many companies are struggling to even offer health insurance coverage.

There are certain benefits employers are required by law to provide. These include:

- Providing time off to vote, serve on a jury and perform military service.

- Complying with all workers' compensation requirements.

- Withholding FICA taxes from employees' paychecks, as well as paying the employers portion of FICA taxes.

- Paying state and federal unemployment taxes, thus providing benefits for unemployed workers.

- Contributing to state short-term disability programs in states where such programs exist.

- Complying with the Federal Family and Medical Leave (FMLA).

Any benefits provided above and beyond the above list are completely at the discretion of the employer, but chances are your employer will offer at least a small menu of benefits to you. Some benefits, such as paid vacation, come at no cost to you, while others, such as health insurance, may be subsidized by your employer but may also require you to pay a portion of the cost as well, should you choose to enroll.

At the start of your employment, you should carefully consider all of the benefits offered by your employer, making sure that you understand each one and how it can impact you. It's okay not to take advantage of benefits you feel are of no use to you – free child care, for example, if you don't have children – but remember that ignoring certain benefits – like retirement plans in which your employer matches your contributions – is like throwing money away. Following are descriptions of several of the more common types of employee benefits.

Vacation and Sick Leave

It's pretty much a given that your employer will offer you some form of vacation and sick leave. To begin with, you will most likely receive a few paid holidays a year, like Christmas Day, Thanksgiving Day, Fourth of July, and maybe a few others.

Depending on your employer, you may also receive paid vacation time, although at the start of your career you probably won't have much. At most companies, the amount of vacation time an employee receives depends on the length of time the employee has worked at the company. For example, employees with one year of service may receive one week of paid vacation, while an employee with 10 years of service may receive three weeks.

U.S. employers also, according to the Department of Labor, offer an average of nine paid sick days to employees. These are days that can be used during an illness or for scheduled doctor health-related appointments.

Today, more companies are implementing a "Paid Time Off" system for paid leave, in which employees accrue days off over time that can be used for any purpose the employee chooses. For example, in a Paid Time Off system, employees might earn 8 hours (or one work day) per pay period of paid time off. If there are 26 pay periods per year, an employee earns 208 hours per year, or 26 days of paid time off to be used as the employee chooses – for vacation, sick time, or other reasons.

Health Insurance

In this age of exorbitant medical costs, health insurance is what most employees name as the most important benefit provided by an employer. Health insurance offers medical benefits covering most of the care doctors and nurses provide. Sometimes health insurance also includes dental and optical coverage – usually at a small additional cost. These programs may also provide health care support to an employee's children or other dependents. Some plans allow the employee to have health insurance even after he/she retires. Common types of health insurance plans include:

Health Maintenance Organizations (HMOs)

HMOs are groups of physicians and other health professionals who have agreed to offer their services for a fixed fee, paid by the insurance program and the patient, usually in the form of a co-pay of as little as $10.00. HMOs are generally less expensive than other options, but restrict your choice of health care providers to those participating in the plan. If you choose to see a provider not participating in the plan, the cost of your care is not reimbursed. HMOs also require referrals for care beyond your primary care physician and may have more stringent limits on the kinds of care you can receive.

Preferred Provider Organizations (PPOs)

As with an HMO system, PPOs have a list of medical service providers, commonly referred to as "preferred providers." You are encouraged to choose a provider on this list, but you also have the option of choosing a provider that is not on the list. When medical care outside the PPO system is chosen, participants are reimbursed at a lower level. These plans are usually more expensive, but offer more flexibility in the care you receive and may not require referrals.

Fee-For-Service Program

Although not as common as the previously mentioned health care options, the Fee-for-Service program allows participants to choose their own medical provider. Participants are then reimbursed for medical care services after they are received. Oftentimes, there are set payment amounts, or deductibles, such as $200, before a participant will be reimbursed for medical costs. There may be other plan requirements including shared payments for medical services and prescriptions and a maximum amount of medical costs the plan will cover in a lifetime.

If your employer offers health insurance, you should enroll. Although you may be young and healthy, illness, health conditions and accidents can happen at any time, and one extended illness, injury or hospital stay can cost tens of thousands of dollars – putting you in debt for years to come. That being said, you don't necessarily have to enroll in the most expensive option available. Weigh your options carefully and choose the insurance program that fits your needs, but don't pay for additional services and benefits that you don't need.

Disability Insurance

Disability insurance provides financial support when an employee becomes injured or ill and is unable to do his/her job. The two types of disability insurance are short-term and long-term.

Short-Term Disability Insurance
Short-term disability coverage often begins right away if an employee is in an accident, or it may begin within a few weeks of an illness or some other disability. For example, this coverage would provide a portion of the employee's salary to someone hurt in a car accident who needs a few weeks off from work to recover. In addition, some short-term disability policies cover time away from work for pregnancy and the weeks after giving birth.

Long-Term Disability Insurance
Long-term disability coverage is offered by employers less commonly than short-term disability insurance. This type of insurance provides benefits to an employee when a long-term or permanent illness, injury, or disability makes it impossible for the employee to continue to perform his/her job duties. Long-term disability benefits often last until retirement age.

Some states also offer disability insurance and require employers operating in that state to enroll employees in the programs. If this is not the case in your state, you should still consider enrolling in disability insurance, even if it is at an added expense to you. Though it may be unlikely, a short period of disability can cost you your financial security for years to come. The added expense of purchasing disability insurance through your employer is usually minimal – and can save you a lot of money and stress in the future should you encounter a situation where you are unable to work because of a disability.

Life Insurance

Your employer may also offer free or low-cost life insurance plans. The main purpose of life insurance is to provide financial support to an employee's family in case of death. The beneficiary of a life insurance plan is usually a relative such as a parent, spouse or child. Life insurance pays a lump sum benefit to the beneficiary of the policy after an employee's death. If you are not currently providing support to any dependents such as a spouse, child or elderly or dependent parent, you may find it unnecessary to enroll in your employer's life insurance plan, especially if it is at an additional cost to you. However, if you have dependents, life insurance is always a good idea.

Retirement Programs

Retirement plans are savings and/or investment plans designed to develop a fund to be used to provide you money to live on in the years following your retirement. Although your retirement years may seem a long way off, don't ignore the value of starting early when it comes to planning for this time in your life. Not convinced? Consider the following example

Recent Graduate	Not So Recent Graduate
• Begins investing for retirement at age 21.	• Begins investing for retirement at age 30
• Invests $2,000 each year until she is 29 and does NOT invest any more money for her retirement after that.	• Invests $2,000 each year and continues to do so until she is 65.
• Total contributions: $18,000 at a 10 percent compounding rate of return.	• Total contributions: $70,000 at a 10 percent compounding rate of return.
• Value at age 65: $839,556	• Value at age 65: $598,253

The moral of this example: **If your employer offers a retirement program, take advantage of it!**

Typically, retirement plans offered by employers are contribution plans. This means that participants make contributions to individual investment accounts; the resulting benefits are based on the contributions plus their earned interest. Depending on the kind of plan offered by your company, your employer will contribute to your plan or you will have to contribute your own money to the fund, which may or may not be matched by your employer. The most common forms of retirement programs include:

401(k), 403(b) or 457 Plans

The names of these plans refer to the section numbers of the Internal Revenue Code that authorizes them. The primary difference between these plans is who can offer them. For example, private companies offer the 401(k) plan, whereas the 403(b) and 457 plans are offered by non-profit, tax-exempt organizations. Regardless of the type of organization you work for, the plans are very similar. Your employer selects different investment options for you to choose from. Usually, the investment options vary in terms of risk and aggressiveness. With these plans, you will contribute your own money to the fund, which may or may not be matched by your employer. One benefit of these plans is that they are portable, meaning that you can take the money with you (with some guidelines) should you decide to change employers.

Profit Sharing Plan

With a profit-sharing employee retirement plan, your employer makes contributions that may vary from year to year based on the company's profitability. If your employer makes contributions to a profit-sharing retirement plan, these contributions and earnings accumulate tax-free until you withdraw them. This type of plan cannot be transferred and applied to the retirement plan at your new employer, but can be transferred to your own personal retirement account.

Employee Pension Plans

In the past, pension plans sponsored by employers or labor unions were typically "defined benefits plans" in which a specific dollar amount for each year of service to a company was provided each month to the employee upon retirement, regardless of contributions. For example, a company might provide $100 per year of service. An employee with 30 years of service would then receive $3000 per month upon retirement. Like the profit sharing plan, these plans are not portable – meaning that when you leave the company, you could not take your accumulated benefits and apply it to the retirement plan at your new employer. However, you can set up your own personal retirement account to have the funds transferred to.

Educational Assistance

Educational assistance programs usually provide full or partial reimbursement of employee expenses for books, tuition, and fees associated with advancing or maintaining their level of education. In other words, you can go to school to earn education that will advance your career – on your company's dime! Most likely, your employer will require that the education support your current position or another position at the company (an accounting firm, for example, will pay for employees to earn their CPA, but won't pay for an employee to attend nursing school), and may require that you attend specific schools.

Transportation Subsidies

Many companies, especially those located in cities, offer employees assistance with transportation by providing free or reduced cost bus or train passes, shuttle services, carpool assistance services, or free or reduced-cost parking. Often, cities or states will provide incentives to companies to do so, in an effort to reduce traffic or emissions. If your company offers transportation benefits, you may be able to commute to work for free on your city's subway system, receive free shuttle service from the bus station to the front door of your office, or be matched with co-workers who live near you and would be willing to share a ride to work.

Alternative Work Schedules

More and more companies are offering alternative work schedules to meet both their own and their employees' needs. Alternative work schedules allow employees to work outside of the traditional 9 to 5, five days a week work schedule and create a work week that works for them. Employers, as well, may like alternative work schedules and arrangements because they can reduce overhead (fewer employees in house, fewer desks needed, less electricity used), increase coverage (employees working odd hours are there to answer the phones), and increase productivity (fewer missed days because employees are happy and able to attend to their lives outside of work). Some common alternative work arrangements include:

Flextime

Flextime gives employees the flexibility of choosing the hours they will work – usually within the limits set by their employer. For example, an employee taking advantage of flextime might work four ten-hour days instead of five eight-hour ones, and take Fridays off. Or an employee who needs to be home early to care for children coming home from school might choose to work from 7 a.m. to 3 p.m. instead of the typical 9 to 5 work day. Flextime is great for employees who have special circumstances (like children or a second job), or who just like the flexibility of working when they want.

Telecommuting

Telecommuting is becoming so commonplace that it actually has its own trade organization! Quite simply, telecommuting is working from home, using technology like the Internet, e-mail, phone and fax to communicate with the office. While not all work circumstances make telecommuting possible (a nurse, for example, can't provide care from home!), those positions where an in-person presence is not necessary are becoming increasingly more "off site" positions. Even those who don't telecommute on a regular basis may occasionally take advantage of telecommuting – on days when a child is home sick or on a day when they must be at home to let a plumber in but don't want to miss a day of work. While it sounds attractive, telecommuting does come with its own set of pros and cons, and isn't for everyone. Many telecommuters cite lack of human interaction as a downside of working from home, while others lack the self-motivation to get their work done without the structure of an office. If your employer offers telecommuting, consider very carefully whether you have the personality to be a productive telecommuter.

Job sharing

Job sharing is exactly what it sounds like – sharing a job. In job sharing, two people fulfill the requirements of one job by dividing the work week and work functions between them. This arrangement is perfect for working parents, people who are completing an educational degree, or those who have other jobs, hobbies or circumstances that make working a 40-hour week difficult. Job sharing does, however, require a good partnership and good communication between the job sharers.

Other Benefits

Every company has its own menu of benefits. Some are more extensive than others, but don't count out the small benefits your company may offer. Things like free health screenings and flu shots, reduced-cost gym memberships, free educational seminars on both work subjects (i.e. an "Effective Management" seminar) or non-work subjects (i.e. a "File You Own Taxes" class), or reduced cost services at local vendors like dry cleaners, restaurants or travel agencies are commonly provided by employers – and can add up to hundreds or even thousands of dollars in savings over the course of a year. Check out what your employer offers!

Chapter 15

Employee Rights

You'll likely spend the early days of your employment learning the ropes – there are many rules, policies and standards to learn. But you should also know that there are rules, policies and standards that your employer must follow as well.

The Federal government and your state government both have laws designed to protect the rights of workers. Your company will likely also have policies, rules and protocols in place to help reinforce existing laws and to help create a positive and productive work environment. But even if your company doesn't state in a written policy that they are against discrimination, harassment or that they provide unemployment insurance for their employees, they still must follow federal and state laws that provide these kinds of protections for workers. As an employee, you are entitled to the following rights:

- **Discrimination Protection** – It is against the law to discriminate during hiring and firing or while considering job performance, salary or promotions on the basis of age, gender, race, disability, medical condition, national origin, religion or creed. Some states also protect you from being discriminated against on the basis of sexual orientation or even your weight.

- **Harassment Protection** – You are generally protected from being harassed verbally, physically or sexually while on the job.

- **Safe Work Environment** – Employers must provide a safe working environment for employees and must provide compensation insurance to cover medical and disability costs should an employee be injured or become ill due to something that occurred on the job.

- **Unemployment Insurance** – Employers must pay for unemployment insurance to cover unemployment benefits to workers who are fired or laid off.

- **Wages Protection** – There are laws and protections in place to ensure that workers receive a minimum wage and fair wages for overtime work.

- **Job Protection** – In most cases, your job is protected should you need to take leave to attend to jury duty, military service, have had a child, or because you are ill or must care for a child or parent.

- **Breaks** – While no federal law requires employers to offer breaks to employees, many states as well as industry standards require that employers make bathroom facilities available, and allow employees to take time to use bathroom facilities, eat, and rest from duties.

- **Whistleblower Protection** – You are protected by law from being fired for reporting your employer for breaking laws (or "blowing the whistle").

- **Personal Information Protection** – Your employer is only allowed to obtain certain information about you and can only use it to make judgments of you on a certain basis. This information includes credit history, criminal record, medical information, prior salary, and personal information such as your marital or parental status, age, or religious or philosophical beliefs. For example, a potential employer can ask if you have ever been convicted of a felony, but cannot ask if you plan on having children.

The specifics of these rights are quite extensive and may differ from state to state and industry to industry, so spend some time familiarizing yourself with the laws, standards and regulations that apply to your position and the industry you will be working in. The Internet is a great resource for locating this information. The following pages also highlight a few of the common questions and concerns regarding employee rights.

If You Get Sick

It happens to nearly everyone. From something as harmless as a cold to a condition as serious as cancer or as long term as multiple sclerosis or AIDS, most people will become ill or be injured at some time during their career and require leave from their job. Some people may even become ill or injured due to something on the job.

The bad news is that there is no federal law requiring your employer to give you paid sick time or unpaid leave unless you have a disability or are covered by FMLA, the Federal Family and Medical Leave Act. The good news is that most employers provide employees with sick time to give them time to recover from illnesses or injuries. Depending on the company, the number of sick days allowed varies, as do other related requirements and restrictions. For example, you may be required to furnish a doctor's note to prove your illness, you may lose your sick days if you don't use them within a certain amount of time, or you may only be able to "save up" a certain amount of sick days to use at a later time. Be sure to familiarize yourself with the details and specifics of your company's sick leave policy.

If your benefit package comes with sick days, your employer should not stop you from using them or threaten you with punishment or termination if you use them legitimately and follow company policy. However, you can legally be punished or terminated for abusing your company's sick policy or for taking a sick day if you are not provided with sick days as part of your employment agreement. But it may be illegal to fire you if your injury or illness falls under FMLA or disability laws, even if sick time is not part of your benefit package.

FMLA provides American workers the right to take up to 12 weeks of unpaid leave per year to attend to serious medical conditions. You must have worked for your employer for at least one year, your employer is entitled to a doctor's certification that your medical leave is necessary, and, if possible, you must give at least 30-day notice of your intent to take leave (this may not always be possible in the case of medical emergencies). Leave does not have to be taken all at once (you may, for example, take a few days per month for chemotherapy treatments). FMLA leave can also be taken to care for a sick child or parent.

While your employer is not required to pay you during your leave as part of FMLA, your job will be protected and you cannot be terminated during your leave. If your employer employs fewer than 50 people, however, it is not required to adhere to FMLA standards.

If you are injured or become ill due to the circumstances of your job, you most likely are eligible for Workman's Compensation Insurance. Workman's Compensation Insurance – often called Workman's Comp. – will generally cover all of your medical expenses, wages lost while you are sick or injured, and any job retraining or training that you might need to prepare you for your return to work or to help you change positions should your injury or illness render you unable to return to your prior position. Usually you will receive about two-thirds of your normal salary while on Workman's Comp., but because this compensation is not subject to taxes, it will probably be about equal to what your paycheck is after taxes.

Your company maintains a Workman's Compensation Insurance policy that covers all of these costs. At the start of your employment, you should familiarize yourself with your company's policies and coverage – such as what you need to do and what things you need to document should you be injured or become ill, and how much coverage you will receive. That way, if you are injured or get ill, you will know what to do and will have less to worry about at an already stressful time.

Maternity/Paternity Leave

Whether planned or unplanned, a pregnancy should not interfere with your current employment or career status.

Maternity and/or paternity leave is the time a mother or father takes off from work at the birth or adoption of a child. Unfortunately, paid maternity or paternity leave is not commonly offered by U.S. employers, though that is changing as more and more progressive companies realize the benefit of offering this kind of leave to their employees. Employers who offer paid maternity and paternity leave often find that they are able to attract and retain high quality employees by offering this benefit, and that they enjoy more productivity and loyalty from employees who have been given adequate time to care for a new child before returning to work.

Even if your employer does not offer paid maternity or paternity leave, you can still take time off to care for a new child without losing your job. FMLA, as described earlier in this chapter, gives employees up to 12 weeks of unpaid leave to care for a new child. You also can use a combination of your employer provided sick time, short-term disability, and vacation time, all of which will be paid, as well as unpaid leave to cover the amount of time you would like to take off to care for your new child. Every employer has different rules regarding what kind of leave and how much leave you can apply to maternity or paternity leave. Therefore, you should familiarize yourself with your company's policies, even if you don't plan on having children any time soon.

Sexual Harassment

Sexual harassment has been a hot topic in recent years but most people do not fully understand the issue. Sexual harassment is defined as the unwelcome sexual conduct of a supervisor, colleague or client. This sexual conduct could include sexual comments, pressure for sexual favors, unwelcome touching, sexual jokes, the display of degrading sexual material or even sexual assault. Anybody can be sexually harassed – male or female, young or old, overtly attractive or otherwise. However, to be truly illegal, behavior must fall under the two definitions of sexual harassment that are recognized by the courts.

- **Quid Pro Quo Sexual Harassment**
  In this kind of sexual harassment, an employee is discriminated against, denied promotions or raises, or is subject to other consequences because he or she refuses the sexual demands of a supervisor or colleague. For example, if your boss asks you on a date but you decline and are then demoted as a result, this may be quid pro quo sexual harassment.

- **Hostile Work Environment Harassment**

  In this kind of sexual harassment, unwelcome sexual conduct in your work place is so pervasive that it negatively affects your work environment and causes your work to suffer, even if you are not a direct subject of the sexual conduct. For example, if two male co-workers are constantly telling sexual jokes for all the office to hear and the boss does nothing, despite the conduct being brought to his or her attention, this might be hostile work environment harassment.

While conduct that falls under the definitions of quid pro quo or hostile work environment harassment is the easiest to legally prove as illegal sexual harassment, the U.S. Supreme Court stated in a 1998 ruling that any sexual conduct that a "reasonable person" could determine was causing discrimination in the workplace could be defined as sexual harassment. In other words, even though behavior may not be explicitly quid pro quo or hostile work environment, you may still be able to prove in a court that the behavior was sexual harassment.

To curb sexual harassment and to avoid legal ramifications, many companies have implemented strict policies regarding sexual conduct at the office. For example, to discourage any appearances of impropriety, your company may make sexual relations between employees a behavior that is punishable by termination, or it may have strong consequences for employees who tell jokes or stories of a sexual nature. Many companies also have training programs in place to teach employees what sexual harassment is and how and why it should be avoided. You should make sure that you understand your company's policies regarding sexual harassment – so you can understand when a supervisor's or co-worker's behavior has crossed the line, and so you can be sure that your behavior doesn't. If you believe that you may be a victim of sexual harassment:

- Keep a record of occurrences, including any messages or e-mails that can document the behavior.

- Make your harasser aware of his or her behavior and ask him/her to stop. Even better, write a letter demanding that the harassment stop and keep a copy.

- Obtain a copy of your company's sexual harassment policy and reporting system so that you can follow your company's procedures.

- Take your complaint to a superior or to your human resources department, if applicable.

- If reporting the harassment to your employer does not stop the harassment, look into reporting the harassment to the proper government or law enforcement agency, or hiring an attorney.

Sexism, Racism, Favoritism

Maybe you suspect that your boss doesn't like you. Maybe she gives other employees better assignments, pays them more, or promotes them above you – even though, in your opinion, you deserve it more. Is this discrimination? Maybe. Is it illegal? Maybe not.

If your boss simply likes another employee better than you and acts accordingly, this is not illegal discrimination, it is simply favoritism. It's not against the law for a supervisor to like one employee more than another, to find certain employees annoying and treat them accordingly, or to think one employee is more qualified than another because he shares the same alma mater as the boss – no matter how unfair or unethical it may seem.

If you suspect a supervisor is playing favorites, you can take it to human resources, but they don't necessarily have to do anything about it. On the other hand, many companies have policies discouraging this kind of behavior, and may have systems in place to ensure that employees are not victims of favoritism.

For discrimination to be illegal, an employer must negatively single out employees or potential employees on the basis of their protected class – which includes race, color, religion, creed, sex, national origin, age (older than 40), disability, veteran status, and sometimes (depending on state law) sexual orientation, marital or parental status, or weight. Legally, employers cannot discriminate on the basis of the above reasons in any aspect of employment, including:

- Hiring and firing
- Compensation, assignment, or classification of employees
- Transfer, promotion, layoff, or recall
- Job advertisements
- Recruitment
- Testing
- Use of company facilities
- Training and apprenticeship programs
- Fringe benefits
- Pay, retirement plans, and disability leave

If you suspect that you are the victim of illegal discrimination, ask yourself the following questions:

- Are you a member of a protected class?

- Were you fully qualified for your position? In other words, were there any other legitimate reasons for the adverse action taken against you?

- Was a negative action taken against you? For example, were you fired?

- Were you treated differently than an equally qualified person who isn't in your protected class?

- Did managers or supervisors regularly make rude or derogatory comments related to work and directed at members of your protected class? For example, "Women don't make good engineers."

- Is there a history of discrimination at your company?

- Is there a noticeable lack of diversity at your company?

- Have you noticed that other employees in protected classes are singled out for negative treatment?

- Are there statistics that show favoritism toward or bias against any group at your company (for example, 99 percent of managers are male)?

- Did your employer violate well-established company policy in the way it treated you?

- Did your company hire or promote less-qualified, non-protected employees in the same job?

If the answer is yes to many of these questions, you may be a victim of discrimination.

Your first step should be to exhaust your options within your company. If you believe your supervisor or another superior is discriminating against you, your company may have policies and systems in place to handle your grievance fairly. Familiarize yourself with the discrimination policies at your company (which should be outlined in your employee handbook or on your company Web site), then see your human resources department or representative to discuss the issue or make a formal complaint. Depending on how your company handles discrimination complaints, you may be removed from the chain of command of the accused supervisor or department, asked to document your complaints so that action can be taken against the accused, or be asked to participate in mediation.

If you feel that you did not receive adequate or fair treatment from your employer or if you believe that your entire company is guilty of discrimination, you can go further. You can hire an attorney to advise you of your rights and the merit of your case, and to represent you in legal actions against your company. If you don't want to or are unable to hire an attorney, both Federal and state governments have agencies designed to investigate discrimination claims against employers.

The Equal Employment Opportunity Commission (EEOC), headquartered in Washington, D.C., is the federal agency responsible for investigating discrimination claims against employers. EEOC district and area offices are located throughout the country and you can find one in your area by checking your phone book or Internet listings. However, if your employer is small, with fewer than 15 employees, your rights are not protected by the EEOC. Instead, you should contact your state's fair employment practice agency, which you also can find in your phone book or Internet listings.

Jury and Military Duty

Most states have laws requiring employers to give workers unpaid leave to attend to civic duties like voting, jury duty and military service. Some states even require that this leave be paid by the employer.

Whether or not the law requires it, the Bureau of Labor Statistics reports that 87 percent of all employers do pay employees for time missed to attend to jury duty. You should familiarize yourself with your state's laws regarding jury duty, as well as your employer's policies about leave needed for jury duty, but, generally, you cannot be penalized or terminated for missing work to serve on a jury. If your employer threatens to take action against you because you have missed work due to jury duty, you probably have the legal right to challenge this.

As with jury duty, if you are called to serve in the military, most states require your employer to provide you unpaid leave and re-employ you without any loss of benefits, status or reduction in pay once your service is completed. This includes situations where you are drafted, are called to service as part of a national guard or reserve unit, or must complete regular training as part of your military duties.

Each state has its own specific conditions and requirements concerning lawful leave for military duty, and individual employers also may have additional requirements or even benefits regarding employees who must take a leave of absence to serve in the military (for example, they may pay you for the first 90 days). If there is a possibility that you may be called to serve your country, you should make sure that you understand your state's laws and your employer's policies regarding military leave.

Job Descriptions and Office Protocol

As a new and inexperienced employee, you are probably eager to prove your abilities and reluctant to say no to any task your supervisor assigns you. But you should know that, while being agreeable and a team player will definitely work in your favor, being a yes-man who gets walked all over is not a requirement. So how do you know when what your boss is asking of you has crossed the line? And how do you say no and still save face?

Most companies would frown on supervisors using company resources (namely you) for personal gain. You have been hired and are being paid to perform functions and complete work that benefits your company and fulfills its mission – not to address your boss's holiday cards or pick his kids up from soccer practice. In some cases – if you work for the government or some other publicly funded body, for example – it may even be considered an illegal misuse of public resources.

That said, depending on your job function, there are sometimes legitimate reasons for doing things outside of your job description that personally benefit your boss. If, for example, your boss is on deadline to complete an important report that everyone in your department has contributed to, and she asks you if you can pick lunch up for her so she can continue to work through her lunch hour, you'd be pitching in for the good of the company by getting her a sandwich. You'd also likely be considered a colossal jerk for telling her it's "not in your job description." On the other hand, if your boss sees you as nothing more than a personal gopher and you find yourself spending more time on her personal matters than on the responsibilities for which you were hired, she's most likely abusing her power, breaking corporate policies, and taking advantage of your inexperience. Your boss's requests are probably crossing the line if:

- The duties are performed on your own time, with no compensation.

- Your supervisor asks you not to tell anyone else about the chore.

- You end up working extra hours to complete your own work because you've spent so much time on personal favors for your boss.

- You find yourself having to explain to others how you are spending your time and why you are performing the tasks that you are.

- You are ever asked to do something unethical, illegal or in violation of other employees' rights or privacy.

If you find that your boss is taking advantage of you, the best tactic is to explain to the offending party clearly but diplomatically that, while you are happy to help out, these extra jobs are taking you away from the primary responsibilities for which you were hired. If that doesn't work, you may have to discuss your complaints with someone higher up on the chain of command, or with someone in the human resources department.

Remember that, as an entry-level employee, you may not always be given the most desirable tasks. You will probably become well-acquainted with the copy machine, the fax machine, the filing cabinets and the phone system during the early years of your career. You may even be asked to make the coffee or go pick up lunch. That's okay – this is a time to prove yourself, develop your understanding of the work world, and create a place for yourself at your company. But, you also have a right to be treated fairly and your company likely has policies in place to make sure that you are.

Workplace Abuse

You probably remember the schoolyard bully from your elementary school days. Unfortunately, the schoolyard may not be the last place you encounter this unsavory character – bullies can be found in work places as well.

While physical violence and abuse is rare, research indicates that one in five workers is a victim of emotional and verbal abuse. Some experts estimate that the cost of workplace abuse is high – nearly $200 million in lost productivity, health consequences, employee turnover, and general workplace dysfunction.

By some accounts, workplace abuse has increased in recent years due to the stresses of modern life, including dual income families, longer work weeks, added duties and fewer workers, commuting ills, and so on. As a result, more and more companies are putting policies in place to define workplace abuse and establish clear ways to curb it. Your company likely has an employee handbook that outlines which behaviors are acceptable and which are not, as well as the potential consequences of engaging in unacceptable – or abusive – behavior.

Most states do not have specific laws regarding abuse in the workplace; however, the same laws that protect you in your home and in public are also in play in the work place. If a colleague or supervisor behaves in a way that would be defined as illegal in the world at large, then what they are doing is abusive and should be reported to those in charge at your company, and possibly to authorities as well.

Even if the bad behavior of a boss or co-worker is not defined as illegal, your company may have policies in place that prohibit it. For example, calling someone stupid or cursing at them isn't necessarily illegal or punishable by law, but your company may not allow your boss to do these things without repercussions.

Don't think that because you are new, inexperienced, or young that you have to put up with bad behavior, insults or threats. Even if the person abusing you is your superior or boss, you do have recourse. Familiarize yourself with your company's policies regarding employee behavior and the systems in place for reporting abuse. It can also be useful to keep a record of abusive behavior as it occurs so that you can document a pattern of abuse.

And, of course, if at any time you feel physically threatened or in danger of any kind, remove yourself from the situation immediately and report it to both your employer and the authorities.

Chapter 16

Unemployment

Unfortunately, the chance of being laid off or fired at some point in your career is becoming more likely as companies struggle to stay in business. Therefore, it's in your best interest to take appropriate actions now to avoid the risk of being unemployed. This chapter covers how to avoid being laid off or fired as well as methods to recover from unemployment.

How to Know if You're Going to Lose Your Job

Most people will say that being laid off or fired came as a complete surprise, but the truth is that this career-altering event seldom happens completely out of the blue. In fact, there are many solid clues that indicate you are close to losing your job – you just have to know what to look for. These clues don't necessarily seal your fate as one of the legions of unemployed, but if you notice more than a couple of these happening where you work, you may want to prepare yourself.

Clues You May be Laid Off

- How are your competitors doing? Are other companies in your industry experiencing layoffs, bankruptcies or other difficulties? If so, it may be a bad sign for your company as well.

- What is your company's financial status? For example, has the company lost a big client or contract lately?

- Is there a lot of talk of cutting costs and budget cuts? Is the company in a hiring freeze? Has there already been a round of lay-offs somewhere in the company?

- Is your company at the center of negative news articles or a scandal?

- Have you noticed that bills from suppliers and service providers are being paid late?

- Has your paycheck been late or "bounced"?

- Have managers and other higher ups been resigning? If so, this could be a sign that they know something negative about the company that you don't know.

- Are a lot of normal expenses being cut back – travel, expense accounts, support staff, supplies?

- When people quit or are fired, does your company assign their duties to other existing employees rather than hire new employees to replace them?

- Has your company changed hands, been bought out, or completely replaced its management?

Clues You May be Fired

- Are you in constant conflict with your manager?

- Is your manager documenting his/her interactions with you more regularly and in more detail – creating a "file" on you?

- Have you received a poor performance review, failed to meet performance goals, or been put on "probation" or a performance improvement plan?

- Are you being left out of "the loop"? In other words, are you being left out of information, meetings, projects and events that you normally would have been a part of?

- Have you made a major mistake or misstep that you suspect could cost you your job? Everyone makes mistakes, but sometimes a mistake is so big that it cannot be overcome – even if it wasn't completely your fault.

- Have you been told that you have a bad attitude?

- Have you been passed over for a raise or a promotion that you expected?

- Are some of your job functions being reassigned to others?

- Have others at your same level in your company been sent to professional training or given perks that you have not?

- Does it seem like people are avoiding you? Are co-workers harder to get on the phone? Does your supervisor avoid looking you in the eye? Has your office been moved to a more remote location? Those may be signs that people are distancing themselves from you because they have heard that you are about to be fired.

- Have you been asked to train a new employee in exactly your job functions, but not because you need help or are about to be promoted? You may just be training your replacement!

The Indispensable Employee

So you've caught wind that big lay-offs are heading your way. Now what? Make yourself an indispensable employee – one that your company can't live without. It won't necessarily ensure that you won't be laid off eventually, but you'll most likely be one of the last to be hit, giving you ample time to line up your next opportunity.

Of course, you shouldn't just develop these characteristics because you fear you might be laid off – these are general traits that make a great employee, so they can also make you more promotable, more likely to get a raise, more trusted and respected at your job, and more satisfied and successful overall.

- **Get the Skills** – The rule is the more you know the better off you are. Even being the only one who knows how to perform a mail merge, un-jam the copier, back-up the computer system, or create a spreadsheet can add up in a manager's mind to someone whose skills are essential. Learn as much as you can and use your knowledge to help your company.

- **Become an Expert** – Concentrate on what you're good at and develop an expertise on that subject that's unrivaled by anyone else at your organization.

- **See the Big Picture** – Understanding how your job functions and your department's work fit into your company's big picture can help you be more efficient and effective in your work. And, because you understand how the company works, you are adaptable to other job functions, making you a valuable company asset.

- **Volunteer** – Volunteer to help wherever you can and take on any project you think you can excel. Knowing that you're a go-to person who is willing to take on all projects – big and small – can make you essential and hard to part with. Just be sure not to overextend yourself – taking on so much that you can't do your work well will only serve to push you to the front of the lay-off line.

- **Think Outside the Box** – Someone who is creative, can come up with new solutions to old problems, and who brings new and exciting ideas to the table is always essential.

- **Communicate Well** – Communicating well is an essential and valuable skill in just about every field. If you can speak well, write well and generally represent the company professionally, you will be seen as an asset.

- **Be Positive, Well-Liked and a Team-Player** – Difficult people are usually the first on the chopping block when it comes to lay-offs – even if they are more educated, skilled or experienced than their more likeable and appealing co-workers. Having a good attitude, being friendly, and being willing to work on a team all make you easy and fun to work with – an asset that will help you avoid being one of the first to go.

- **Document Your Success** – Keep a folder of your successes so you can prove just how valuable you are to the company if you should need to. Keep a tab of clients you have landed, money you have saved the company, projects successfully completed, your ideas implemented, and other job achievements. Don't be a braggart, but make sure those in charge know about your successes – by copying them on key memos and e-mails and keeping them informed of the status of your work.

- **Be Flexible** – In times of crisis, companies look for employees who can roll with the punches. Employees who can take on new job functions, put in extra hours, or adapt to new and changing corporate culture and expectations fit the bill.

- **Cut Costs** – Lay-offs usually mean that your company is in crisis – and cost-cutting mode. If you can prove that you and your work save the company money, rather than cost it, your job will be all the more safe from cuts. Does your job function increase production, land new paying clients, help reduce wasted time, effort or resources? Figure out how your job adds to the bottom line. And if it doesn't, figure out a way to make sure that it does.

- **Be a Self-Starter** – Managers operating in a lay-off environment are stressed – so anything you can do to reduce this stress will be seen as a plus. Employees who need constant supervision, feedback and direction are usually the first to go because managers figure that they put so much effort into maintaining the employee's work that they might as well do it themselves. Try to succeed in your work with as little hassle to your manager as possible – the more independently you can work the better.

- **Understand that Relationships Count** – Being friends with the boss doesn't guarantee that your job will be spared, but it's a fact of life that who you know counts. That doesn't mean that you should start brown nosing the boss or run a popularity contest in the office, it just means that networking, office face time, and creating meaningful work relationships is important.

What to Do if the Unthinkable Happens

If you are fired or laid off, there are things you can do to minimize the damage of your unemployment and to start the search for a new job successfully. In fact, you should familiarize yourself with the tenants of "successful unemployment" and create a strategy for what you will do should you be laid off or fired – long before it actually happens to you. Even if being laid of or fired is the furthest thing from your mind right now as you embark on your new career, you should plan for the worst to avoid being caught completely off guard.

- **Participate in the Exit Interview** – It may sound about as appealing as a root canal, but an exit interview can be a valuable experience – both for you and your former employer. During an exit interview, you can voice your opinions about your employment – and you might even be able to glean some information about how you can be a better employee at your next stop on your career track. Just be sure to take the high road. Tempered honesty is fine; tactless complaining is not. You may hate your boss, but telling the HR rep during your exit interview that he is a complete jerk won't do anyone any good. Letting them know that you could have used more constructive criticism and realistic deadlines might help them guide your former manager to a better management style.

- **Always Keep Your Resume Current** – Even if you think that being fired or laid off is a remote possibility, you should keep your resume up to date. Make it a monthly habit to update your resume, develop your list of references, and add to your portfolio of work. You never know when that unexpected job offer may come your way.

- **Leave on Good Terms** – Even if you are fantasizing about insulting your boss and telling off the nosy receptionist, abstain from doing so. Don't do something that you might regret once your emotions have calmed – you never know who you might encounter later in your career.

- **Ask for a Recommendation Letter** – Even if you have been fired, you probably know someone at your company who would be willing to serve as a reference and/or write a recommendation letter for you. Ask for it now, while you and your performance are still fresh in this person's mind and while you are still in daily contact.

- **See if You Have a Severance Package** – Some companies offer employees generous severance packages – especially if they have been laid off. If you are eligible, spend it wisely – it may be all you have to get you through to your next job.

- **File for Unemployment** – Your employer has been paying unemployment insurance on your behalf during your employment, and you are now eligible for the benefits. Don't let your pride stop you from taking this important step. You don't know how long you will be unemployed, and your unemployment checks may be a big help financially. Contact your state unemployment office to find out what you are entitled to and how to collect.

- **Contact Your Creditors** – If you have student loans, personal loans, a mortgage, car loans, or credit card debt, you should contact your creditors to let them know that you have lost your job and may have difficulty making payments for a short amount of time. Many creditors have programs in place to help customers through unemployment, and allow reduced payments, deferment of payments, or at the very least may agree to waive late fees or finance charges or hold off on reporting late payments to the credit bureaus. A good offense is the best defense when it comes to creditors – make the call before they start calling you.

- **Check out COBRA** – The Consolidated Omnibus Budget Reconciliation Act (COBRA) gives employees who have lost their jobs the right to choose to continue their employer's group health insurance for a limited period of time, at the employee's expense. In other words, if you lose your job, you don't have to lose your health insurance. Even though you will have to pay the premium cost yourself, you can continue to subscribe to the same health plan that you had while you were employed, usually for up to 18 months. Although the several hundred dollars you might have to come up with each month may seem hefty, you are better off continuing your healthcare coverage than not. If you get ill or injured and do not have health insurance, your healthcare costs can be in the thousands or even tens of thousands – a debt that can take years to overcome. By law, your employer should provide you all the information you need to continue your healthcare insurance coverage through COBRA.

- **Evaluate Your Financial Situation** – This is the time to make a budget and stick to it! Assess how much savings you have and budget that money to last you for as long as you can.

- **Consider it a Job** – Make job hunting your new vocation. Set aside a place in your home as a "home office," set your alarm each morning and "go to work." Devote as much time to job hunting as you would be devoting to a job, if you had one. That means eight hours a day, five days a week – and some overtime if necessary. This is also the time to practice your interviewing skills, capitalize on your network of contacts and brush up your resume and cover letter writing skills.

- **Keep Stress in Check** – Losing a job is stressful, whatever the circumstances. It can also be embarrassing, expensive, time consuming and frustrating. Keep stress at bay by keeping it in perspective. Stay positive by viewing your unemployment as a time to revaluate your career goals, revitalize your commitment and passion for your profession, and reignite your career.

- **Prepare Your Script** – You may feel like keeping your unemployment a secret, but it's not a good idea. Being honest and letting people know that you are unemployed and looking for a new job is one way to get the word out that you are available for hire. You'd be surprised at how many people are willing to tip you off on job leads, put a good word in for you, or make a phone call on your behalf when they find out you are unemployed. Prepare a "script" of what you will say to people regarding your job loss so that you are less nervous revealing your unemployment. You don't have to give every gritty detail of how or why you were fired or laid off – just let people know that you and your employer have parted ways and that you are in the market for a new career challenge.

- **Track Your Expenses** – Costs associated with finding a new job can be deducted on your taxes. Check with your accountant about the details, but make sure to save all receipts of any job-hunting expenses as you go.

Chapter 17

Staying Competitive

You've earned your degree and landed your first job. Now it's time to sit back and relax, right? Wrong. The truth is the hard work is just beginning. Your degree and your first job are the foundation for your career – but what you learn and what you do from this point on will be the building blocks to your success.

Today's corporate world is highly competitive and moves fast. If you don't want to get left behind you have to do everything you can to keep yourself valuable and attractive to your employer. That means viewing the world as one big classroom – and gaining as much knowledge, experience and skills as you can along the way. Here's how.

Join a Professional Group

If you thought your days in the clubhouse were over, you were wrong. You probably joined and contributed to social, academic, and athletic groups in the past because they offered you something – friendship, fun, inside information, organized social events, and the potential to learn and experience new things. As a professional, there are similar groups available to participate in, such as professional associations.

Professional associations are organizations that represent people who share a common background in a particular field or industry. These groups provide their members access to networking and social events, professional development activities, and career services. In addition, they may also conduct research about the field or industry; raise money for and organize charitable work that is somehow related to the field; work to attract people to the field by offering college chapters, mentoring or scholarships; or lobby at the state or federal level for legislation that benefits their particular field.

Professional associations also provide these benefits:

- **Camaraderie** – Meet and network with other professionals in your field.

- **Mentors** – It's not uncommon for professional associations to provide an applicant pool for mentors. Some even offer formal mentoring programs.

- **Career Advancement** – You will meet people at different companies and likely get inside information about who is hiring and what you need to do to get the job. Many professional associations even maintain a job board on their Web site or in their newsletter where current openings in the field are listed.

- **Professional Development** – Most professional organizations offer a variety of development opportunities, from educational seminars, to professional training and certification, to mentoring and internship programs. If you want to get specific training and education in your field, your professional association is the place to look.

- **Information** – Most associations maintain Web sites that are full of valuable information. They may also distribute newsletters, reports, magazines, white papers and other publications. A lot of associations conduct research and make the information available to members. Some even have libraries and archives.

- **Experience** – Most professional associations are run, at least in part, by members. As a result, your professional association may give you the opportunity to gain leadership experience by serving the association as secretary, treasurer, president or in another capacity. You can get public speaking experience by offering to present at meetings or writing experience and a publishing credit by authoring an article or column for the association newsletter. Many associations have other volunteer opportunities as well, where you can gain diverse experience.

- **Resumé Development** – You can add your membership in professional associations to your resumé. You can also include any significant work with the association (served as secretary, for example, or appeared before the legislature on behalf of XYZ association). A professional membership is a great way to fill out your resumé early in your career.

If you are interested in joining a professional association and need some assistance in locating one that will meet your needs or requirements, consider the following suggestions.

- **Do Your Homework** – Search the Internet for associations that are relevant to your field and check out their Web sites to see if they offer what you are looking for.

- **Contact Your College** – Speak with your college's alumni or career center as they often work with a variety of professional associations.

- **Ask Around** – Ask your co-workers, supervisors, professors, and others in your field what associations they belong to.

- **Contact the Association** – Most associations have a membership chair you can e-mail, write or call for more information. You'll likely receive a membership packet, with information about the association and its benefits and an application and other necessary materials for membership.

- **Attend a Meeting** – The best way to see what kind of people belong to an association and how it is run is to drop by a meeting. Most will allow potential members to attend one or two meetings before joining. When you attend the meetings, introduce yourself to people at the meeting and inquire about their opinions of the association.

- **Ask for Special Rates** – Though the cost of normal membership should not be prohibitive, many associations offer a discounted membership for new college graduates. If you have the foresight, you should even look into joining a professional association's student chapter before you graduate – many associations will waive initiation costs and other fees for members who were previously student members.

- **Participate** – Just joining an association isn't enough. To get the benefits, you have to participate. Attend meetings, volunteer for committees, leadership roles and other work, and get to know the members.

- **Consider Dual Memberships** – By all means, start with one membership. But remember that there may be several worthwhile associations in your particular field, or that are relevant to your career. For example, there may be a trade organization for your field that you want to join, but you may also consider joining the Minority Business Association or Women in Technology Association.

Get Certified

Professional certification is available in nearly every professional field. In some fields – like nursing – certification at some level is mandatory. In others – like public relations – it is completely voluntary. Certification, especially if mandatory, is sometimes offered through government agencies, but is more often offered through professional associations or college programs.

Certification usually requires candidates to take a series of classes, seminars or lectures and pass one or more exams that test their knowledge of their profession. Certifications may also require you to have a certain number of years of service in your profession, may mandate that you volunteer hours of service, and may require ongoing education and testing to maintain your certification. Certification provides a number of benefits, including:

- Helping employers evaluate potential employees during the hiring process.

- Motivating employees to continue their professional development and stay up-to-date in their field.

- Giving consumers a way to judge the expertise and credibility of service providers (for example, consumers should choose a contractor to renovate their home who is a Certified Master Builder, as certified by the Homebuilders Association of America).

- Helping employers evaluate employee performance and set performance goals (for example, your raise or promotion could be contingent on receiving a specific accreditation).

Even if certification is not required, there are many good reasons to pursue certification in your field. Certification will help you stay up-to-date on the latest advances, research and ideas in your industry; it will demonstrate to your employer and others that you take your profession seriously and are committed to growth and learning; it will help you develop new skill sets, knowledge and talents; and it will inspire you, motivate you and help you set both short-term and long-term goals for your career and professional development.

Continue Your Education

The most successful professionals understand that staying competitive in their jobs and in the marketplace means continually learning new skills and information, from running the latest software, to mastering the latest management philosophies, to acquiring the accounting skills it takes to run a multi-million dollar department.

After graduation, it's understandable that you may need a short break from studying. But don't rest on your laurels for too long. Committing to learning demonstrates to your employer that you are willing to learn and open to new opportunities – plus it helps you acquire skills and knowledge you need to do your job better and advance to more challenging roles. And you don't necessarily have to pursue a PhD to learn what you need – one-day seminars, six-week classes, even an hour spent at a lecture will add to your expertise. Provided below are just a few options to consider to obtain further education:

- **Community Colleges** – Community colleges offer both credit and non-credit classes. You can brush up on your business writing skills, learn a new language, try your hand at graphic design, get certified in computer programs, learn the latest management strategies – and more. You won't earn a degree, but you'll learn a lot.

- **Colleges and Universities** – Perhaps you have decided that what you need to succeed is another degree. Check out area colleges and universities for available options.

- **Trade or Vocational Schools** – There are trade and vocational schools for just about every skill. For example, there are secretarial schools where you can learn shorthand and keyboarding, technology schools where you can get computer skills, and culinary schools that offer classes in event planning.

- **Professional Associations** – As outlined earlier in this chapter, professional organizations can offer certification programs, professional development seminars, and a variety of other learning opportunities. Check out networking groups, trade organizations, and specialty professional clubs like women's or minority business societies.

Although continuing your education can be very rewarding, before you decide to proceed you should consider the following suggestions to ensure you make the most of your investment.

- **Choose Wisely** – You may be interested in art history, but will acquiring an in-depth knowledge of Baroque art help you get ahead at work? Learning for the sake of learning is great, but if your time is limited, make sure what you are learning is interesting, enriching – and likely to boost your career.

- **Aim High** – You may be a copywriter now, but you probably have your sights set on something bigger. Don't just think about what you do now – think about what you want to do tomorrow. If you are a copywriter but want to be a project manager, think beyond taking more writing classes and consider taking management, business or technology classes that will help you acquire the knowledge and skills you will need to be the manager you want to be.

- **Consider Your Schedule Carefully** – Most continuing education institutions today offer classes at all times, including early morning, evening and even on the weekends. Pick the schedule that fits your lifestyle and remember that you will likely spend at least two hours studying and completing class work for every hour you spend in class.

- **Consider the Costs** – Unfortunately, learning takes money, and as a recent graduate, finances may be tight. Check out every possible avenue to fund your continuing education – scholarships, student aid, bank loans, personal loans from family – and even your company. Many companies offer tuition reimbursement to employees who successfully complete education that will help them do their jobs better.

Volunteer and Lead

Everyone knows that volunteer work can have a meaningful, positive and lasting impact on communities, families and individuals. But did you know that volunteering can also have a positive effect on your career? In fact, volunteering can:

- Provide you an opportunity to establish contacts, build your network and foster mentors. The leadership of the groups you volunteer for can even serve as excellent references or provide valuable recommendation letters.

- Give you a platform to demonstrate your talents, skills, commitment and leadership. You may not be a manager at your job yet, but volunteering to manage projects and people at a charity can prove that you are up to the task.

- Serve as an important part of your growing resumé. There's no rule that says that every item on your resumé has to be a paid position.

- Give you the opportunity to learn new skills, gain new knowledge, and experiment with different interests and roles.

- Help you practice the skills you need to succeed in your career, giving you experience and self-confidence. Not sure you can deliver a high-impact project on a low-cost budget? Try it by volunteering for your favorite non-profit agency. When you succeed, your confidence will soar – giving you the courage you need to take on more challenging projects and roles at work.

- Expose you to different perspectives and experiences, helping you to appreciate diversity – an important life and career lesson.

So, you want to volunteer. You know there are an endless number of organizations that need your time. But how do you find them? Consider the following:

- Contact your local government, United Way, colleges, or churches and synagogues and ask them to make recommendations.

- Visit your city, county or state Web site. Many list local and regional volunteer opportunities.

- Search the Internet. There are a variety of volunteering Web sites that post volunteer opportunities or even match volunteers with organizations.

- Think about your interests and how you have been helped in the past. Were you a member of the Boys & Girls Club as a child? Do you remember being tutored by a volunteer at the library during middle school? Maybe you attended the summer arts festival of a local non-profit arts organization each year. All of these groups likely have volunteer opportunities – all you have to do is ask.

After you've done your research and know who needs your time, keep in mind the following suggestions to make the most of your volunteer time:

- Don't overextend yourself. It's better to be realistic and commit two hours per week than to try and commit 10 hours per week and not be able to follow through. You may not get paid to volunteer, but it's still a commitment – take it seriously.

- Find volunteer opportunities that help you make the most of your skills and talents – or help you acquire new ones. Licking envelopes for a charity fundraising direct mail is fine, but writing the copy for the direct mail piece is even better – especially if you are trying to earn more prime writing projects at work. Figure out how you can use your volunteer time as a way to build your resumé, not just spend your time.

- Volunteering is a great way to build your resumé, but it's not the only reason to give your time – you should also enjoy yourself and feel that you are making a real difference. When it comes to volunteering, find a cause you are passionate about and believe in – otherwise the responsibilities you take on will be just another thing to add to your To-Do list.

Chapter 18

Networking

You've probably heard the saying – "It's all about who you know." However, a better statement is "It's all about who knows you." This has never been truer than at this time in your life. Developing a group of contacts, mentors and business contacts – who know you – is one of the most important things you can do in your early career. How does this happen? Networking.

Networking is essential to your growing career, and will remain a vital part of doing business over the course of your professional life. Networking makes you more visible; helps you meet people who can be valuable to you; helps you gain vital professional information about organizations, people and trends; and generally gets you out in the world so that opportunities don't pass you by. However, networking doesn't necessarily come naturally – especially for those who are shy, lack confidence, or find it difficult to meet people. Networking, like any other skill, must be developed to make the most of your opportunities. Here's how.

What is Networking?

Quite simply, networking is the act of meeting people with whom you can develop mutually beneficial relationships and exchange information, advice, contacts or support. A few examples of networking might include:

Example 1

You attend an industry cocktail party and begin a conversation with an executive at Company X. You know for a fact that your company would love to do business with Company X. During the course of your conversation, you mention an article that the executive expresses interest in reading. At the end of the night you and the executive exchange business cards. On Monday, you e-mail the executive a link to the article that you discussed. A few weeks later, the executive e-mails you to let you know that his company is looking for the services of a company just like yours to help on a specific project. You let your manager know the information you have received. Your company submits a proposal and wins a big contract – and you get big points with your manager.

Example 2

You attend the monthly meeting of your industry trade organization and meet several young professionals in your industry. After giving one of these young professionals a tip on a great restaurant to take clients to in her area, she invites you to have lunch next week with her and several of her colleagues from a company with similar interests as your. You begin to have lunch on a regular basis with this group. A few months later, a job opening that is a perfect match for your skills and talents opens up at their company. Because of your inside information and a few good recommendations from your lunch group, you land a new job – and a $7,000 pay raise!

Example 3

While attending an industry educational seminar, you make small talk with other attendees during the morning break. In the course of one conversation, one attendee mentions that his daughter is trying to get into the very same college that you attended. You offer to have lunch with his daughter to coach her on what she needs to know about the college – and he offers to introduce you to his best friend, who just happens to be a top-level executive at a company that you would like to sell your product or service to.

You will notice one thing that all three of these stories have in common – both parties gained something out of the exchange. This is the true spirit of networking: an exchange of some commodity that results in benefits to both parties.

Why Network?

Networking isn't always easy, but it's important. Networking in the early stages of your career can help you land jobs, secure promotions, develop your understanding of your profession, and gain important insight into what it takes to succeed in your field. As your career progresses, networking will likely remain an important activity, as it provides professional insight into clients, sales leads, potential business opportunities, and career advancement potential.

Networking isn't just something you should do – it's something you *must* do to succeed. The good news is that it's really not all that difficult. If you are a friendly, open individual who likes to meet people and help people out if you can, you've already met most of the criteria of a networking pro.

How to Network

So how do you build your network? First, determine who can help you. Start with what you know, including:

- **Your College** – Many schools have alumni associations that are great places to network, or even offer lists of alumni who are willing to speak with other alumni about professional opportunities.

- **Family** – Think beyond your parents and be sure to consider your cousins, aunts, uncles, etc.

- **Family Friends** – Include your parents' friends and business associates.

- **Advisors and Supervisors** – Include your former professors, teachers and coaches. Also include your past employers, like your summer internship boss.

- **Members of Groups You Belong to** – Including clubs, churches, teams, associations.

- **Your Friends** – Just don't stop at your immediate friends; be sure to include your friends' parents and family, and people they know (maybe your college roommate's father works for a company you would like to do business with, for example).

Next, research additional opportunities for networking, including:

- **Professional Groups** – Trade organizations, industry associations, professional clubs that you can join.

- **Educational Opportunities** – Seminars, classes in professional skills, educational speeches, forums and talks.

- **Networking Organizations** – There are organizations that meet on a regular basis with the sole purpose of establishing a place for people to network!

- **Volunteer Work**

- **Social Opportunities in Your Field** – Gallery openings if you work in the art field, grand opening parties of stores if you work in retail, or holiday open houses at companies you are interested in.

Finally, develop a sound strategy for networking:

- **Have a Great Elevator Speech** – An elevator speech is a synopsis of who you are and what you want people to know about you that can be delivered in the time that it takes to ride an elevator a few floors. Figure out what is important about you and boil it down to a minute or less.

- **Don't Forget Your Tools** – Always bring business cards and even copies of your resume wherever you go.

- **Be Engaging** – This includes being friendly, confident, open and interesting. Make sure you are up to date on the latest industry trends and current events so you have something to talk about.

- **Be Interested** – Develop a genuine curiosity and interest in other people and what they have to say. No one likes a person who monopolizes the conversation by talking about themselves – plus, if you never take the time to get to know others, you'll never know what they have to offer you.

- **Drop Names** – Take advantage of who you know by letting people know if you have friends or colleagues in common.

- **Build Relationships** – People are more likely to stick their necks out for you if they feel they have a relationship with you. Don't ask for anything specific right off the bat. Instead, take some time to build the relationship and see what develops. If you ask for a job right away, the person might say no – and be turned off. If you stay in contact over the course of a few months through e-mail, lunches and meetings, you might be the person who naturally comes to mind when a job opens up.

- **It's a Two-Way Street** – If you go into networking only focused on what's in it for you, you'll come up empty handed. Networking means that both parties help each other. In other words, you have something to offer as well. Spend some time thinking about what you have to offer. It could be information, contacts, skills, or even emotional gratification.

- **Keep Track** – Develop a system of tracking your networking contacts. Keep your business cards in a binder, update your Rolodex on a regular basis, and add contacts to your e-mail address book. Don't lose a valuable contact because you misplaced her business card.

- **Be Respectful** – Remember that people are trying to be nice – don't abuse their kindness. Ask permission before passing on their contact information, don't call excessively, and don't act as if you are always looking for a favor.

- **Be Grateful** – If someone does something nice for you, thank them! E-mail is fine some of the time, but don't underestimate the power of a written note. Depending on how extensive the help was, you may even owe someone a lunch or a gift.

- **Keep at It** – Networking isn't something that stops when you get to a certain point. Just because you landed the job, the client or the contract, doesn't mean that you can cut your networking ties. Don't let good contacts and good networking go to waste because you don't take the time to maintain your network. E-mail, write and see your contacts on a regular basis. You never know what kind of great things might pop up – or what kinds of things you can do for other people.

Chapter 19

Mentors

You've got your business cards, your briefcase, your power suit and your job. What else do you need to succeed? Try a mentor.

No doubt you have had people in your life who you have admired for their skills, talents or personalities. Whether it was a trusted professor, an older student at your college, or a friend or relative who had experienced the same challenges as you, you probably asked these people for advice, tried to follow their example, and used their success as a way to pave your own path to the top. Whether you (or they) knew it at the time or not, these people were mentors to you – and probably a contributing factor to your success.

Mentors Defined

Mentoring is a one-to-one relationship based on encouragement, constructive criticism and feedback and a mutual willingness to learn and share. Simply put, a mentor is an experienced and trusted advisor who is successful in his/her profession and has the ability and willingness to teach and assist others.

Typically, the mentor is more experienced than his/her protégé. The protégé is usually someone trying to move up professionally and develop his/her career. The relationship benefits both participants The protégé receives professional advice, guidance and nurturing. The mentor gets the opportunity to strengthen his/her leadership skills and the good feeling of knowing he/she is helping someone on the path to career success.

Having a great mentor can be one of the most enriching experiences of your career. Why? A mentor can:

- Help you set long-term career goals and short-term work objectives.

- Help you understand your organization, your profession, and how you can use your skills and talents to excel within them.

- Help you identify professional problems and create strategies and solutions for dealing with them.

- Provide honest and useful feedback and criticism.

- Be the gateway into successful networking by giving you valuable contacts, invitations to industry events, and information and recommendations on networking in your profession.

- Provide advice and guidance on how to accomplish your career goals.

Making the Most of Your Mentor

Many companies offer mentoring programs to assist employees to find a mentor. Some companies even require new employees to participate in a mentoring program, to help ease their entry into the corporate culture. Programs like these will usually require you to fill out a questionnaire about yourself, your goals and your working style, then will match you with a more experienced employee at the company who is a good fit with your personality, experience and needs.

If your company has a mentoring program, by all means participate. If your company does not have a mentoring program, you might also look into your alumni association, trade organizations in your industry, or professional groups in your area, as many of these kinds of groups also provide mentor programs. If, however, you don't have access to a formal mentoring program, you can still develop a great mentoring relationship. In fact, most mentoring relationships are informal.

When seeking a mentor, consider carefully what kind of person would help you in this capacity. A good mentor is someone who:

- Is established and respected at your company and/or in your profession.

- Understands your company's or industry's corporate culture.

- Has skills, experience, or talents that you admire and would like to develop.

- Has goals and a career path similar to your own.

- Is familiar with your position and the tasks/projects you work on.

- Has good communication skills – including good listening skills.

- Is willing and able to devote the time and effort necessary to develop a good mentor relationship.

- Is flexible, positive, empathetic and encouraging.

- Can relate to and get along with you, but is different enough from you to be able to stimulate your thinking and creativity and offer you something you can't learn on your own.

Now that you know what kind of person you are looking for, how do you find him/her and start the relationship?

- Develop a list of qualified candidates and rank them in order, beginning with the most qualified.

- Consider supervisors or managers at your company, work friends, acquaintances from professional organizations, past professors of subjects in your field, even previous employers.

- Develop a letter explaining that you are seeking a mentor and that you feel he/she would be a great mentor. Outline what benefits you expect to receive from having a mentor, as well as what you believe your mentor will gain from the relationship. Also include what expectations you have in terms of time requirements. If you have a relationship already established with your chosen mentor, it may make more sense to use this letter as a list of talking points during a one-on-one conversation rather than sending the letter.

- Provide your potential mentor with your resumé so he/she can evaluate your background.

- Let your potential mentor know that you would like to meet to discuss a possible mentoring relationship, then meet for lunch or coffee. If he/she is unable to serve as your mentor at this time, ask if he/she can recommend someone else with similar experience.

- Try to explain to your potential mentor why being your mentor will be a worthwhile experience, but never pressure someone into being a mentor. To be a great mentor, a person must be enthusiastic and committed – and someone who has been pressured into taking on the responsibility is probably not the best candidate.

- Set up a schedule for meetings (you'll meet on the first Tuesday of every month, for example) and a timeline of goals you would like to accomplish with your mentor.

Once you have your mentor, make sure to make the most of your relationship:

- Respect your mentor's time. Your mentor is making time for you in his/her busy schedule. Don't be too demanding of your mentor's time, and make sure you are always prepared for your meetings and arrive promptly.

- Be prepared. When you meet, have a list of professional issues you would like to discuss, as well as questions and/or work you would like to share.

- Be professional. You and your mentor may become good friends over the course of your relationship – but you should do your best to keep the mentoring time professional. During mentoring meetings, avoid discussing personal matters.

- Stay open-minded. You have asked your mentor to provide you guidance, advice and feedback. Make sure you are open to his/her comments and avoid being defensive.

- Provide your own feedback. Let your mentor know if their guidance or advice has helped you master a skill, finish a project successfully, or earn a promotion.

- Be grateful. After every meeting send a note or an e-mail thanking your mentor for his/her time. If you meet over lunch or coffee, pick up the tab. If your mentor's help results in a great promotion, raise or other recognition, you may even consider a small gift. And, if your mentor works at your company, consider letting his or her boss know just how much you have been helped by copying the boss on a letter or e-mail of thanks.

- Make the relationship a priority. Don't let your mentoring relationship stagnate because you feel you don't have time or energy. If you find that scheduling becomes an issue, discuss alternate arrangements with your mentor. And remember that this relationship is important to your career and deserves all the time and effort you can contribute to it.

Chapter 20

Getting Ahead

You've probably heard the term "climbing the corporate ladder." It implies that your career involves taking several small steps up in order to reach your professional peak. However, as you have learned throughout this book, establishing a successful career involves much more than climbing a few steps. It takes initiative, established goals, a lot of work and can be a bit of a balancing act.

To get ahead you need to become a self-promoter. Learn to market your skills and accomplishments, and know how and when to ask for career and salary promotions. The following sections outline strategies and provide suggestions and tips on how you can get ahead in your career.

Get Noticed

You may not work in marketing and sales, but you still need to market and sell something every day: yourself. Some people are naturals at tooting their own horns, while others cringe at the thought. Some people – we've all known the teacher's pet or office braggart – even cross the line into narcissism. It's a fine line to walk between modesty and boastfulness, but getting it right and selling yourself with confidence can make all the difference in your career.

Television commercials sell products by showing their value to the customer and highlighting how they are new, different and better than other similar products. You need to do the same for yourself. What is your value to your co-workers, your manager, your company? How are you different or better than others? What makes you stand out? Now, how do you get other people to notice? Here are a few tips for getting noticed – without crossing the line:

- **Be Your own Biggest Fan** – Exuding confidence is the first step toward getting noticed. If you start every conversation with *"This is probably a stupid idea, but..."* chances are people will agree. If you slouch, bite your nails, and generally look unsure of yourself, people will doubt your abilities. If you are modest to a fault, deflecting compliments and telling people you don't deserve your success (*"It really wasn't a big deal"* or *"Anyone could have done what I did"*), they'll believe you! The first person who needs to believe in you is you. Once you've mastered that, you can get everyone else to believe in your abilities, too.

- **Participate in Meetings** – Meetings are a great opportunity to demonstrate your knowledge, skills and creative thinking. Don't talk just to talk, but if you have something to say or to contribute, don't be shy. Many meetings include management and even top-level leadership or owners. Make the most of your meetings by coming prepared, paying attention, and contributing when you can.

- **Expand Your Social Circle at Work** – You'll never get noticed if only one or two work friends know how great you are. Think of your office as one big pool of potential contacts and act accordingly. Meet and greet people from all departments, volunteer to serve on multi-department projects, get to know people from all areas – from the receptionists and the IT staff, to the accounting staff and upper management. The more people you know, the more chances you have to show your value.

- **Do What No One Wants to Do – and Do it Well** – Every company has that task or project that no one wants to take responsibility for – and that has been brushed to the side time and time again. Maybe it's the employee recognition program that's never gotten off the ground, a news clipping portfolio that's never been organized, or marketing for a little known service that's never been developed. Whatever it is, take it on and take it to new levels of excellence. It may not be the most appealing or fun project, but performing well on a task no one else wants to touch will foster management's confidence in your abilities and commitment, and can lead to prime projects in the future.

- **Get Credit Where Credit is Due** – If you do something great, let it be known, and known to those who count. It's fine to call you mother and let her know that you've made a client happy – she'll be proud. But what you really need to do is let your supervisors, co-workers and upper-level management know. Copy supervisors and projects teams on letters and e-mails that state a job well done from clients with a note saying *"Thought you might like to see this good piece of news."* Issue memos under the guise of "keeping management informed" about projects that have been successfully completed, costs that have been cut, and problems that have been solved.

- **Give Credit Where Credit is Due** – Make sure you give compliments and kudos to co-workers when they contribute. Being known as someone who supports other people has a positive impact; plus, if you are generous with compliments others will be too.

- **Keep Track** – Keep an ongoing file of complimentary e-mails and letters and a "score sheet" of successful projects, tasks and solutions you have been part of. This file will be useful during performance reviews, when you are being considered for a promotion, or on days when work is getting you down and you need to be reminded of your victories. While you are at it, keep your resume up-to-date with your achievements and ask for recommendation letters when the time is right.

- **Keep it Positive** – Making yourself look good by making others look bad isn't only bad manners, it's a bad idea altogether. It may work for a while, but people will catch on. Earn your success through your own good effort, not through the mistakes or shortcomings of others.

Excel at Performance Reviews

Performance reviews are used by organizations to evaluate the value of an employee, provide the employee important feedback on job performance, and to make decisions about raises and promotions. Performance reviews make many employees nervous and anxious, but they don't need to. If you are a good employee, all you need is a little careful preparation to ace your performance review.

Performance reviews are different at every organization, but a few general kinds of reviews include:

Probationary Review

Probationary reviews are what they sound like – they either precede or end a "probation" period. This probation period could be the period of time – usually 30 to 180 days – that some companies take to evaluate new hires before extending permanent, full-time employment. Or, it could be a period of time used to evaluate employees who have performed poorly in the past and are facing termination if improvements are not made. A probationary review can be performed at the start of a probation period to outline what is expected of the employee, or at the end of the probation period to evaluate how well the employee has met those expectations.

Annual Review

Annual reviews are the most common way that companies evaluate employee performance. The main focus of an annual review is to evaluate and highlight an employee's performance over the past year, develop strategies to improve the employee's performance, discuss short-term and long-term career goals, and determine if the employee is eligible for a salary increase of promotion. An annual review is also a time to let the employee know that he/she is not meeting company expectations.

Semi-Annual Review

Although not as common as the annual review, semi-annual reviews are used for the same purpose but are performed more often.

Self-Evaluation Review

Some organizations require employees to conduct a self-evaluation prior to a performance review. This ensures that the employee has considered and evaluated his/her performance and provides supervisors with a brief synopsis of his/her accomplishments, areas in which they need help or improvement, and goals for the coming year.

No matter what kind of performance review format your company uses, there are things you can do to prepare. And the important word here is *prepare*. Don't make the mistake of thinking you can go into a performance review without preparation and simply answer questions off the cuff. To truly have a successful – and useful – performance review, you must put some time, thought and effort into it. Make sure your performance review is a positive experience by doing the following:

- First and foremost, remember that performance reviews are useful to your company, but they also benefit you. The only way to learn, grow and develop your career is to receive honest feedback and develop plans for ongoing improvement. It may be difficult to listen to criticism – but it will only serve to make you a better employee and a better person.

- At least one week before the performance review, develop a summary report of your accomplishments. This report is similar to a resumé, but outlines and highlights what you have achieved at your company in the time period that is being reviewed. Make sure you include all relevant information, but keep it as brief as possible – a page or less. The format for this report is similar to the Raise/Promotion Request Report sample located in the next few pages.

- Compile documents that support the claims in your summary report. These documents can include letters and e-mails from clients, certificates of completion from continuing education programs, a portfolio of work, or budget statements that show costs cut and money saved.

- If your company uses a format or form for performance reviews, review ahead of time and decide how you will respond to each area or question. Identify any areas of concern and pay special attention to how you will formulate your answers to these areas.

- Remember that image counts. Make sure you dress professionally on the day of your performance review – even if it falls on casual Friday.

- Be prepared to take notes during your review. Your notes may prove to be helpful as you create a plan to improve, and taking notes will demonstrate that you are taking the review seriously and are open to recommendations.

- Avoid being defensive, making excuses or arguing. Remember that part of your review is receiving criticism. No employee is perfect and everyone has room to improve. Try to view your supervisor's criticism as helpful and positive.

- Use the time to self-promote. Your review is a time to identify areas of improvement, but it can also be a time to demonstrate to your supervisor all the areas in which you have excelled.

- Thank your supervisor for taking the time to thoughtfully evaluate your performance and make recommendations. This will show that you value his/her feedback, opinions, and time.

- After the review, go over any documents your supervisor may have provided you, review what occurred during the meeting, and develop a strategy for how you will improve your performance in the areas that have been identified as needing work. Then, share your plan with your supervisor and be sure to document the steps you take to execute this plan. That way, you'll be prepared for your next performance review!

Asking for a Raise

Receiving a great performance review creates a perfect opportunity to ask for a raise. But even a top-notch review doesn't guarantee that your supervisor will show you the money. Ensure that your request is honored by:

- Evaluating your value. Take stock of your achievements, your skills and talents, and your contributions. Compile as much tangible proof of your value as you can. In fact, you may find it helpful to develop a report similar to the one discussed in the previous section. A sample of this report, and an introductory memo, is located at the end of this section.

- Doing some research. Find out how much others in similar job situations and positions are making and how much someone in your position can normally expect to receive as a raise. Many career Web sites list average salaries for a broad range of careers.

- Picking the right time. If you know your supervisor always gets anxious before the weekly management meeting, don't ask for a raise five minutes before the meeting is set to take place. In a perfect world, you'd get a raise because you deserve it, but asking when your boss is in a good and generous mood won't hurt.

- Asking for more than you expect to get – but just a little. If you would be happy with a four percent raise, ask for six percent.

- Keeping your feet on the ground. You think you deserve a 20 percent raise – and you might. But if you work at a small company or your organization is going through a budget crunch, you should be realistic and prepared to receive less than you think you deserve.

- Having a plan B. If you are turned down for a raise, take some time to regroup and make a new plan. Maybe more money isn't in the forecast, but how about more vacation time? Or a more flexible schedule? Tuition reimbursement for that class you've been wanting to take? Your supervisor may not be able to squeeze more money out of the budget for you, but he/she may be able to find something else to reward you for a job well done.

Sample of a Raise/Promotion Memorandum

Memorandum

To: Ms. Sally Supervisor

From: Bill Briefcase

Date: January 14, 2007

Re: Request For Promotion To Director of Advertising

I have worked for XYZ, Inc. for 2 years as Assistant Director of Marketing and Membership. The past 9 months, my position has been focused on developing programs to increase advertising revenues for our periodicals. During this time, I have worked hard to exceed our advertising sales goals. In fact, due to my efforts, we have exceeded our advertising sales goals by 117%, providing XYZ, Inc. an additional $3.4 million in revenue.

As you are aware, the Board of Directors of XYZ, Inc. has recently approved the formation of a new Advertising Department, as a result of a financial viability report that I developed. In that report, I described the growing demands on the resources of the Marketing and Membership Department that have resulted in the reduced growth of our membership. In addition, I described how the addition of an Advertising Department would allow the Marketing and Membership Department to reallocate their resources to grow membership by 12% next year.

The new Advertising Department will oversee all advertising sales, promotions and programs. According to my projections, this new department will add an additional $4.6 million of revenue in the first year alone.

I understand XYZ, Inc. is currently searching for qualified candidates to serve as Director of Advertising. I believe my success in developing our current advertising program, as well as my recent EMBA from State University, demonstrates I have the skills necessary to oversee our Advertising Department. Therefore, I request that I be promoted as XYZ, Inc.'s new Director of Advertising.

ATTACHMENTS:
* "Raise/Promotion Summary Report"
* Letter of Recommendation from Mr. Marketing - Director of Marketing, XYZ, Inc.
* XYZ Magazine Media Kit

Sample of a Raise/Promotion Summary Report

BILL BRIEFCASE

PROJECT ACCOMPLISHMENTS

Developed the Advertising Program for *XYZ Magazine*

- Conducted numerous marketing surveys among our readers to develop a complete demographic analysis that enabled us to attract interest among advertisers in our readers.
- Created our media kit (attached) with the assistance of our Graphics & Communications Department.
- Exceeded first year advertising revenue goals by 173% while only using 64% of the budget.

Increased New and Renewal Subscriptions of *XYZ Magazine*

- Organized regional focus groups with the assistance of our Marketing Department to identify key issues to be addressed in *XYZ magazine* that are important to our readers.
- Organized informational luncheon meetings where subscription staff was provided short educational sessions to learn how to close sales, negotiate, and develop goals.
- Worked with Betsy Backpack, Director of New Sales, in organizing an appropriate incentive program for her staff.

Created XYZ, Inc.'s Management Retreat

- After identifying the need for better communication among departments, I met with department heads to create an outline for how our organization can communicate more effectively. Management then participated in a two-day retreat that I organized to review the outline for a more effective communication program. The retreat was successful in developing our current communication program. In addition, management has requested the need for additional retreats to discuss other organizational issues.

EDUCATION & TRAINING

- EMBA, State University. Areas of focus include Advertising, Marketing and Entrepreneurship.
- Attended the Time Management and Effective Marketing Seminars conducted by the Association of Young Professionals.
- Current Member and Chair of the New Member Committee for the Association of Advertising Professionals.

GOALS

With my direct involvement in the development and overall success of *XYZ magazine's* advertising program, the successful completion of my EMBA, and my dedication to the overall success of XYZ, Inc., I believe that I am an excellent candidate for the new Director of Advertising position.

If you enjoyed *Backpack To Briefcase*, be sure to also read:

ISBN: 097009445-0
Size: 6 X 9 Inches
Pages: 176
Chapters: 18

Your Financial Future
A Guide to Life After Graduation

Your Financial Future is the only financial advice guide developed specifically for the recent graduate. Comprised of key financial information, tools, and resources recent graduates need to establish a successful future; readers will develop financial goals, take control of their debt, learn the costs and benefits of credit, create a budget, determine what types of insurance they need, become an informed investor, find the best bank for their needs, learn if purchasing a car or home is right for them, understand how taxes work, protect themselves from identity theft, plan for their retirement, establish a plan for their estate, and much more.

Learn more about this book and other **Life After Graduation** products and services by visiting:

www.LifeAfterGraduation.com

Life After Graduation, LLC
PO Box 11205, Bainbridge Island, WA 98110
Ph: (877) 569-9816 Fax: (206) 780-7837
Info@LifeAfterGraduation.com

Notes